The "W" Word

Other Books by Jo Horne

Parkinson's Disease for Dummies
(co-authored with Michele Tagliato, MD)
Home-Sharing and Other Lifestyle Options
(co-authored with Leo Baldwin)
The Nursing Home Handbook: A Guide for Families

***

The Winterkeeper
Monica's War

the "W" word

One Woman's Journey
To and **Through**
Widowhood

Jo Horne

**Bucket
Line
Books**

The "W" Word: One Woman's Journey To and Through Widowhood

Copyright © 2023 by Jo Horne

All rights reserved. No part of this book may be reproduced or used in any manner without the prior written permission of the copyright owner, except for the use of brief quotations in a book review.

These are the author's memories, from her perspective, and she has tried to represent events as faithfully as possible.

ISBN 978-1-7337227-4-2 (softcover)
ISBN 978-1-7337227-3-5 (ePub)
Library of Congress Control Number: 2023911902

Cover Design, Layout, and Typesetting by Paul Nylander | Illustrada

Bucket Line Books LLC
Milwaukee • Sarasota

To those who live on,
letting go of the bitter,
celebrating the sweet,
and finding their way.

From the Author

I didn't choose this—no one does.

The first time I filled out a form asking for my status, I automatically colored in the "M" box—as in "married." I was still married, right? After 40+ years, that was still a valid response, right?

But then there was the "W" box—the identity no one chooses as they might choose to marry or divorce or remain single. Widowed is not a choice. It is an identity thrust upon you, and no matter whether you saw it coming (as I did) or not, there's not a damned thing to be done.

And so, you become . . . widowed. You cast off the identity you spent years shaping with another to reveal this stranger—this person who is only half of what they were just a day earlier.

In some ways, I was lucky, I guess. After all I had months to say that final goodbye. But on that December morning, I had no clue how I would ever do that. After eight long years of surviving multiple medical events and crises, my husband and I were told in no uncertain terms that we were coming to the end of one long journey and beginning another shorter but far more challenging one.

For years, his pulmonary hypertension and assorted other health issues had been managed through a combination of medicine, therapies and his own indomitable spirit and will to keep going. We suddenly found ourselves in a whole new place where the doctors spoke in terms of palliative care, comfort care and hospice. We had no GPS for this journey. We had no timeline or schedule—weeks? months? We did know this was the inevitable end of the road—for us as a couple, for my husband as the life force he had been, and for me as his life partner.

Much has been written after the fact by those suffering the death of a spouse or significant other. A good many of those stories have to do with an end that came suddenly. For those dealing with someone in a cognitive state such that they could not participate in those final days, experts often speak of a double whammy—the loss suffered as the person's mental status declined and then, sometimes years later, the actual death. Our story is unique in that we were told. We were given a sort of macabre gift of time to say goodbye.

As a writer by profession, I felt the need to record the journey as it happened. I doubt that I will always be a sympathetic voice in all of this—after all I was not the one facing the end of MY life—although in so many ways I realized afterwards that indeed I was, at least one phase of my life. I suspect there will be times when I will indulge in self-pity and downplay my good fortune to be financially secure and surrounded by support. At such times readers would be completely justified to indulge in the urge to shout, "Snap out of it!", but I will not sugarcoat my story.

From the Author

No matter the circumstances, anyone who has lost a life partner has walked this road. Death does not distinguish when it comes to ethnicity, gender identity, age or finances. My goal is simple—to document my story and perhaps in writing that offer hope and empathy for others. Certainly, I have gained wisdom from others who found their unique way to and through the "W" journey.

How we got here... Day One

EARLY DECEMBER

Here is not a physical place, but rather a physical reality: my husband is dying—as in soon—as in weeks, perhaps months, but definitely not years. Even I, who have been in serious denial throughout, must admit that this is a war he is losing by degrees. I must accept that we have now entered a new normal. I realize that many—perhaps—most widow(er)s-in-waiting do not have the luxury of time to shape that final goodbye. At the end of three interminable days ending with the final devastating prognosis, I understand I am to be given that gift.

Of course, the question is, how will I use this opportunity?

On the eve of that first day of the lead-up to facing the hard reality of our situation, we are at home and have just settled in for the night, blissfully unaware of what the coming days will bring.

On nights when Larry struggles more than usual, I join him in sleeping in our family room—Larry finds sleeping in his recliner aids his breathing. On this night he seems restless and uncomfortable so I bring my blanket and pillow and camp on the sofa. In the pre-dawn hours Larry starts throwing up and that continues every 15 minutes for what seems like days but is in fact a matter of a few hours. That's tough for a healthy body—for him, fighting against two lung conditions and a weak heart, it is catastrophic. Once that finally stops, he rests as I urge him to replace fluids—a losing battle against the dehydration we both know he has suffered. He refuses to allow me to call his doctor or take him to the hospital, so we make our way through the day.

I get it that this is his life and these are his choices to make, no matter how unrealistic I think he's being sometimes. And I get it that expecting him to have empathy for what is going on in my mind is not fair. This is not about me, after all.

But then, why does it feel like it is—at least partly?

As night comes on, he seems somewhat improved. We eat a light supper and watch TV. He takes a call from a friend. I bring him his medications, and we turn in for the night. Despite his objection, I take my place on the sofa.

Around 11:30 he wakes and stirs a bit, but nothing seems unusual. Our family room has by this time gained some of the trappings of a sickroom—something we both hate but understand is necessary. The most offensive addition for both of us is the portable toilet. Of course, such conveniences make life easier, lessening the danger he might try to make it to our bathroom and fall or suffer a dizzy spell, and more importantly maintaining his control over one more piece of his life that is slowly ebbing away. When I realize he is not transferring from chair to toilet as I had expected, I get up.

How we got here . . . Day One

Larry is still in his chair, reaching for something unseen above his head, his fingers opening and closing. His upper body and neck are contorted, his head lolling to one side. His eyes are open but unfocused as he continues to try and pluck something from the air above him. I kneel next to him, my heart hammering. This physical fear and panic are not unfamiliar. We have been here before. More than once. But somehow this feels different. I call his name, but it is as if he has no idea I am there. His hands drop to his lap like dead weights, while he continues to stare up, his eyes darting around as if following a butterfly, his lips moving in some soundless gibberish.

Is this another stroke? My mind races with the possibilities, repeating the mantra that has become my silent prayer: Not yet. Please not yet.

I call 911.

This is a monumental decision on my part. I am risking his anger and disappointment and all the other side effects of making this choice for him. Throughout his eight years battling decline—years that have included three ablations; insertion of a defibrillator; a stroke; a brain tumor—all on top of the sarcoidosis that destroyed 15% of his lung capacity before it was diagnosed and the pulmonary hypertension that we now know will be the official killing agent—Larry has remained adamant about dying at home. His greatest fear seems to be that he will die in a hospital, and so, although we have made many trips to and from, he has vehemently resisted every time.

Thankfully by the time I hear the ambulance siren and hang up with the 911 call center, he seems to be a little more focused. I ask him to squeeze my hands and speak my name. When he does both, I run to open the door and turn on the outside lights for the rescue team, then get dressed for the trip to the hospital while they take his vitals. I grab what I think we might need—his wallet with insurance cards and list of medications; my purse; his glasses; keys. As always, the EMTs are a calming influence, taking charge, getting him stabilized and responsive and into the ambulance. I follow in my car, my mind a blank, my hands gripping the wheel, my eyes riveted on the road ahead, willing the traffic to be light and the lights to be in my favor.

In the ER a team of doctors and nurses focuses on the neuro-piece of things since on the call I had said I thought he might be having a stroke. They take a CT scan of his brain and a routine chest x-ray—the x-ray showing the presence of pneumonia. The CT scan confirms no recent stroke or TIA—good news to be sure, but if not that then what is this? They refer to the incident I witnessed as a possible seizure. Now the emphasis shifts to treating the pneumonia—he is transferred to a regular room and hooked up to IVs for fluid/nutrition supplement and a cocktail of antibiotics.

He is also attached to the usual network of monitors and given oxygen. He seems to be resting or in a state of semi-consciousness unaware of the activity around him. We both know a diagnosis of pneumonia in his state of health is not good.

I settle myself in the chair next to his bed. Someone brings me a blanket and urges me to get some rest. I thank them—each of them—for every small thing they are doing to care for him and for me. I look on every person who comes through the door as the rescuer who might save the day—give us more time. The night and first day pass with a never-ending parade of medical folks in and out. Larry is miserable—basically unable to breathe without oxygen which makes talking nearly impossible. I realize that he is

How we got here ... Day One

really really sick—more so than at any other time. His pulmonologist adds respiratory therapy every four hours. The hospital staff is, of course, focused on controlling the pneumonia—and there is also the possibility that even though he had a flu shot there was a flu virus that caused the throwing up in the first place. Someone tells me the pneumonia was somehow tied to his swallowing back some of the vomit into his lungs—one more graphic detail in the lexicon of his many health issues I would rather not hear.

I wish I were better at asking questions, demanding information. Our friends are very persistent about that—and when I speak to them to update them on Larry's condition, they raise those questions. I have no answers and feel I have somehow failed him—and them. But underneath I ask myself what good would having those answers do. Isn't it a bit like getting a weather report—what one really wants to know is the temperature prediction and will it rain or not? What I really want to know is ...

CAN YOU FIX THIS?

His pain and discomfort are mine as well. Through that night and the next day his pulmonologist stops by to check on him several times, his expression one of concern and frustration—none of the usual banter we have shared over the many years he has been Larry's primary doctor. Beyond the immediate problem of controlling the pneumonia, he is also fixated (as he has been for months now) on trying to figure out why Larry's health has declined so rapidly in such a brief period of time after years of maintaining a fairly steady level of function. His concern and demeanor leave little doubt that he is as worried as I am. Larry has become as much a respected friend as patient.

I wait for his reassurance, but I know he will be direct and honest for Larry has taught him well. He knows that with this patient, he needs to lay out the known and the unknown clearly.

Warning me there is more work to be done—more tests to be run, he reminds me that even before the pneumonia Larry's health was already extremely fragile.

Tell me something I don't know.

I ask him to state the facts plainly, not try and ease me into it.

He hears me and reports that even if they manage to get the pneumonia under control, the toll it will take on Larry's already fragile immune system and compromised lungs will be a heavy one, one that might be impossible to come back from. Further if he has contracted a flu virus on top of the pneumonia that could change the Rx cocktail for treatment and increase the time it would take to see any improvement. Even if treatment is successful for this round, if the pneumonia returns, then the news gets worse.

There is also good news: Larry is responding to the pneumonia treatment although he is still incredibly weak and unable to eat because he simply does not have the energy to do so. Best case scenario (in terms of pneumonia) would be a switch from IV to meds by mouth and, if he could get off the IVs and start eating and drinking, he could be home in a couple of days. Best case scenario for his overall health though continues to be extremely tenuous. After all, as Doc hardly needs to remind me, he has two chronic diseases for which there are no cures plus now this acute crisis.

How we got here—Day Two

GOOD NEWS
The pneumonia continues to respond well to the meds, and the care team has taken Larry off IV therapy and moved him onto oral meds. Also, the EEG showed that the seizure-like event was probably a one-time deal and likely caused by massive dehydration. The prognosis is one more night in hospital followed by discharge with full home-care support in the form of PT, OT and respiratory therapy for the next few weeks. We are both exhausted, of course, and through the day Larry fades in and out in terms of having the energy to talk or visit. I field calls for him while keeping visitors at bay.

His willingness to keep fighting when I know he must be so very tired of it all inspires me. Not once does he chastise me for calling 911, and that tells me that he understands why I felt I had no choice. This trip to the hospital has bought us time, and I know he wants that as much as I do.

NOT SO GOOD NEWS

While the pneumonia is apparently under control and seems unlikely to re-surface, the ongoing decline due to his pulmonary hypertension and flare-ups of the sarcoidosis is undeniable. At this point all the tests that might have shown something that could be reversed and therefore open the door to him being more like his old self and up for his previously limited activity have come back negative. What we are left with is that the underlying cause for his decline is likely neuro-muscular, and we are told that the atrophy of the neuro-muscular structure is not something that can be reversed. The next step—one he would never agree to—would be having a breathing tube inserted.

We have long known that Larry's condition is chronic, progressive and incurable. He remains strong and upbeat and tells me that he has a bit of fight left in him, but adds we need to face some tough realities. I listen carefully and take copious notes as each medical expert explains the situation, preparing to answer the questions I know he will have. But in truth, I do not hear what the doctors are really telling us. There's an old joke about a king trying to decide which of his sons will make the best successor, so he sets a challenge for each. One is sent out among the king's subjects to interact with them while the other is locked in a barn filled with horse manure. When the King speaks with the first son, the young man can do nothing but complain about how selfish the people are and how demanding. With little hope his visit with his second son will be any better, he goes to the barn. There, he finds his son happily shoveling away, singing a song. When he asks how he has remained so upbeat in the face of a task so odious, the boy looks at him and says, "The way I figure it, with all this sh_t, there must be a pony buried in here somewhere."

So, throughout another long day I continue to look for the pony in all the sh_t, reminding myself that every day—every hour—is its own blessing.

How we got here—Day Three

We are home!!!! YAY!!!!

But if I had been in denial before about the full force of what lies ahead, the visit from Larry's pulmonologist this morning to put things in motion for Larry's discharge set me straight. He told us he had ordered palliative care, and I froze. He said the words as if I should have expected them. Yes, I had heard them as a possibility, but possibility meant someday, not today.

I had just begun the process of adjusting to the idea of physical and occupational therapists setting up shop in our already crowded family room a couple of times a week. Now as I listened to this new round of information, my mind struggled to come up with some definition that didn't lead to the final stage—hospice. In fast forward I ran through the five stages of grief in about a minute and a half. Denial, anger, bargaining, depression, and acceptance—okay, those last two would take a while.

After so many incidents where we thought it was the worst, but found a way out, we were being told, not this time.

There are no meds or treatments to fix this.

The doc can't fix it.

I can't fix it.

My rage at the unfairness of it all—of these horrors attacking a man who took care of himself as few do—threatens to overpower me. But then Larry looks at me, takes my hand and says what has become his mantra: *It is what it is.*

As he has from the day he first realized his condition had no cure, Larry takes the news in stride—the man has been ready to die since the day I met him. I don't say that in a morbid way. He just has always been pragmatic about the deal we all get when it comes to life—we get a certain amount and then it's over. There's no calendar for the time or date. Understanding that has always given him the incredible capacity to appreciate each day—and to lose patience with those, especially me, who don't take full advantage of the day at hand and whine about wanting more.

Once the doctor left—his expression showing that he, too, was sad to have to bring such news—the day was a long and emotionally draining one. Once again, a parade of medical folks came and went. Appointments were made. Instructions were given. The toughest part was that everyone seemed to be on the same page in terms of Larry's prognosis.

I wanted someone to disagree. I wanted someone to offer words of hope. I needed that crutch to get me through this initial shock. Larry may insist on straight talk, but I was floundering in rising water and needed something to grab hold of.

Here is the immediate plan of action:

How we got here—Day Three

1. The pneumonia will continue to be treated with meds for at least another week. Thankfully, these are meds he can take at home, and he continues to respond well
2. Starting as early as tomorrow we will have a procession of home care people showing up—a nurse and social worker and hopefully a home health aide to assist Larry with showering and other personal care until he can regain some strength.
3. A week from tomorrow we will be meeting with the pulmonology team and the palliative care team. Larry does qualify for hospice (meaning his prognosis is six months or less) but for now we have opted to go the route of home care to palliative care to hospice rather than jumping straight to hospice.

I guess that's my lifeline. Hope springs eternal.

BOTTOM LINE: no one knows what the coming days, weeks, months may hold. He may indeed find one more burst of strength and stamina; they may come up with some miracle drug. Anything is possible, and we are certainly not giving up—just being realistic. To put this in the sports terms that Larry and I often use to make sense of things: We are in the bottom of the ninth with two outs.

Got that part, but there's still one more out!

PART ONE
The Journey TO

January

The weeks since Larry came home have flown by. At first, he talked about us going to Sarasota for the winter as we have for the last several years. But the first meeting with the home health team put any such idea to rest. We cancelled all the arrangements tied to that starting with rental of the condo. Our landlord who has become our friend insisted that we take back our deposit. The airlines were not as understanding so we lost the cost of tickets. We cancelled the hauler who annually takes our car to and from.

Meanwhile, Larry has become even more obsessed with teaching me what he feels I need to know about finances and quarterly tax payments and such. Never having bought into any sort of online filing system (the man has never so much as turned on a computer), he still maintains everything in carefully organized manilla files in the drawers of a file cabinet next to his desk. On each of those manila folders he has written detailed notes about what the folder contains, who to call if I have questions, and the schedule for whatever might need to be done to keep them current.

Larry and I complement each other in so many ways, but when my propensity to figure something out while staring down the eleventh hour of a deadline comes up against his habit of scrutinizing the information until it is ingrained, we are bound to have some difficult moments. Never known for my patience, I struggle with his need to focus on these mundane details. One of the ways I break away from the hard realities we face is to wander through estate sales or consignment shops. On one such outing, I come across a slender journal—maybe twenty-five pages total. It is blank. I buy it and take it home to Larry.

"I don't care if all you do is repeat the same words over and over again," I tell him when I give it to him that night. "I do not want the only thing I have in your handwriting to be instructions on how to pay the damned taxes."

He laughs. "Deal," he agrees. Then his smile fades. "The real reason I have you watch me do these things is because since the brain tumor, I'm concerned about my math and I want to make sure I get it right."

My heart breaks a little more.

The holidays came and went. I decorated the house. We held a smaller, quieter version of our annual holiday party with friends. We went to see a friend perform in a holiday cabaret, although we left at intermission because of Larry's exhaustion. I arranged for handicapped seating for us at one of the college basketball games that has formed so much of the social frame of our life together. Larry surprised me by having his sister and another friend shop for gifts for me to open on Christmas morning. I made his favorite potato latkes, and we lit the Hanukkah candles.

And on every occasion, I stuffed down the unfathomable truth that it is likely a "last"—that next year this will all be different because Larry will not be here.

Two things about this last holiday season: in my family Christmas was not especially about religion, but rather about the joy of giving—to those less fortunate, to those who had been a special part of our lives that year, and most of all to family. My Dad was Kris Kringle (without the costume and beard). His constant question to Mom as she prepared for the big day was, did she have enough gifts for each of us? His flair for playing Santa extended well beyond our front door. He owned a furniture store, but come Christmas, he ordered a selection of toys—dolls and fire trucks and games, and in a town without a toy store, folks knew Mr. Horne would have the right thing. He once left our Christmas morning celebration to assemble and deliver a bike to a family who called to ask if he still had one available. And when my sister and I helped him wrap the gifts he had bought—or had us buy—for Mom, he always ended the session with a frown that said, "This isn't nearly enough."

So as the pile of gifts grew under our tree, so did the excitement until on Christmas morning the house fairly rocked with exclamations of surprise and delight. We were never huggers or otherwise demonstrative—gift-giving was our way of saying, "I love you."

Larry had no frame of reference for such debauchery. His Jewish traditions were much quieter since Hanukkah is not a major holiday. To him one gift per person seemed more than adequate. In those first years of our marriage, the gift he chose for me was always something practical—something for the house or a heavy sweater or fake fur hat for me to wear over the winter. Having spent most of my life up to that moment in the South, I found it really hard to adapt to the cold of a Wisconsin winter. Often, he would choose his gift when he and I were together, so no surprise on Christmas morning. How I longed for him to understand my need for something more frivolous and spontaneous! Cost was not the issue. I simply wanted to think of him passing a shop window, seeing something there and thinking, "She would love that!" It took a while for me to understand that I wanted what I had seen in my youth—a man who so loved his wife that even with a stack of gift-wrapped boxes ready for under the tree, it was not enough. Call me materialistic and spoiled, and you will be spot on.

And that brings me to the second thing about this holiday season: it took me far too many years to learn and appreciate that "things" lose their appeal after a while. And, of course, if I could trade everything Larry gave me as he adapted to my need for a certain type of holiday celebration for one more day or even five minutes with him, I would gladly do that. Sadly, that time is past, and I will always regret that I wasted so many years focused on STUFF.

STILL JANUARY
To add to the already surreal world that we live in, we awoke today to a swirling snow that looks like we are trapped inside one of those shake-em-up snow globes. Good day to stay in. Thoughts...

The passing days all feel so normal. Larry has insisted I maintain my studio and go there several times a week to write. His oxygen is his constant companion, a mechanical house pet trailing after him. He still makes his own breakfast and lunch, and spends these winter days at his desk, or in his recliner watching sports, news or public television, and at other times reading or visiting with friends who stop by or call. We still go out some, but I do all the driving now. His laughter often fills the house, and he is eager to hear about my day as I prepare our dinner and we spend the evening together.

A friend calls from Florida to say he is planning to come for a visit. People are trying to understand the urgency of the situation, and it's hard to discourage them from coming in spite of the weather. I want to assure them there is time, but I don't know that, do I? The truth is that for now we seem to be in a positive holding pattern—making it even more difficult to accept that this will change. But it will, and I know Larry would far rather see these friends now than later when he is more compromised and perhaps unable to engage. I accept that the time is at hand for friends and family to think about last visits, last goodbyes.

These days we watch our college basketball team's games on TV. For forty years we went to practices and games in person. Our first real date was to a scrimmage in a musty old gym on the urban campus of Marquette University. This team has always been special to us even though neither of us went to school there. So many wonderful memories tied to games and tournaments and kidding around with friends whose loyalty is to a rival team.

The snow also brings back a ton of memories. The first time Larry tried to take me ice skating and my fear of falling would not allow me to let go and enjoy. I realize now that became a kind of metaphor for so much of our life together—my qualms and anxieties preventing both of us from experiencing the full joy of life. I think of the times we went walking on the frozen river near our house, me clinging to his arm, unable to appreciate the thrill of walking on water—albeit frozen. I think of a trip we made to the Outer Banks of North Carolina where there are large sand dunes. Larry took one look at them and yelped like a kid as he half-ran, half-slid down them while I stayed at the top looking for another route that did not involve shifting sands under my feet.

But there are other snow memories like the walks we took at night on unplowed deserted streets. Or the winter we kept snow-blowing the long narrow driveway at our first house, when the snow came so often that we ran out of places to put it. How we laughed when we had to abandon the blower and literally shovel by hand, carrying the full loads to the front or back yards. And always the memory of all those crazy hats and sweaters that Larry bought for me in an attempt to stop my complaints about always being cold. . . .

Then there is the battle of the thermostat: Larry's theory is that one can always dress in layers and keep the house temperature at a steady sixty-eight degrees during the day and lower it to sixty-five at night. My theory is that I should not have to dress like Nanook of the North in my own house. At night as we get ready to go to bed, how he delights in stepping over to the thermostat and turning it down—with sound effects, no less. "Zip-p-p!" he calls out and then chuckles with delight. I pretend frustration. But in truth I look forward to this nightly ritual—as I have come to cherish so many of the little private jokes we've shared over forty-plus years together.

So many wonderful memories to warm us in these dark cold days of the winter we are facing in our lives now. So many memories that will sustain me once he's gone.

NEXT DAY

It's Sunday and because my latest novel is about a Quaker protagonist, I have begun attending the local Quaker meeting. Originally the point was research. After all, for several years now I have been comfortable with my Unitarian faith and was certainly not seeking some sort of new spiritual home. Still, I find the hour of silence enormously healing as I examine my inner thoughts and try to come to terms with what surely lies ahead.

January

Football is definitely on today's agenda. After all, we are in Wisconsin and it's January and there's snow on the ground and crisp cold sunny blue skies above. It's play-off time in the NFL. Larry's sister and her husband arrive to watch the game and have supper with us. We laugh together and bemoan our team's loss, and after they leave, Larry and I read the paper and watch our favorite shows—all so very normal.

And yet. . . .

Is it odd that these days when Larry tells me he's going to take a shower I linger nearby afraid he might fall? It's not as if he's that unsteady. In fact, he continues to exercise daily, and his balance is good and his movements sure, if a little slower. But I have become ever more vigilant, wanting to make sure we have no cause to call the EMTs or worse, make another trip to the hospital. The closer we come to the end, the more I am determined to make sure he has the ending he wants—home, not hospital.

Recalling the night of the seizure, I understand I am unlikely to have much warning when things go south. For this reason, I watch and wait . . . and hope.

Is it odd that I no longer miss going out to see friends or have dinner or go to a film or play? Now people come here and our lifelines to the outside world are those visits, phone calls and our television. And was it only a couple of months ago that I was bemoaning these growing restrictions and yammering on about wanting our life back? About how small our world was becoming? Yet now I savor these quiet evenings at home—just us.

And is it odd that a routine part of my day is to prepare his breathing treatment four times and straighten out the kinks in his oxygen tubing multiple times? And that I approach these tasks as if it were as ordinary as straightening his shirt collar or dishing up a bowl of soup for him?

The "W" Word

At the same time, there is the undercurrent of thoughts that come unbidden and unwelcome at various times throughout the day: who will take care of me? Larry and I did not have children; friends can only do so much; my family is far away and limited to a brother and sister and their spouses.

Thoughts that come while I'm cooking (which I am doing more of these days simply because I am here, and we are not able to go out as we did): what will meals alone be like? When I was in college, a favorite professor died, and I remember going to visit his widow. I have never forgotten that she told me a friend had advised her to never eat a meal standing up—meaning grabbing something and shoving it down while standing at the kitchen sink rather than taking the time to properly prepare food and enjoy it. I don't know how that worked out for her, but I see me grabbing a bowl of cereal (or worse a bag of cookies) and consuming it while running errands or collapsed in front of the TV. With no one to cook for, why would I bother?

Thoughts that come after running errands or being out for some other reason: what will it feel like to come home to … silence? I guess there are tricks I could use, like leaving a radio or the TV on when I leave the house. But whether Larry is here or has gone out for a drive with a friend (or in those "before" days, a bike ride or fishing), there is a presence—the certainty that he will be back; signs that he has recently been there. One can only pretend for so long.

I cannot imagine a life without Larry.
I am frankly terrified.
What will I do?
Where will I go?
WHO will I be?

January

STILL JANUARY? REALLY?

One thing we have lived with for years now is the presence of multiple medications—on the bathroom sink counter and filling much of the space on the kitchen table. Since coming home from the hospital in December we have added an oxygen compressor that runs 24/7, a nebulizer used every four hours throughout the day, and most recently a machine used often by people suffering from sleep apnea to administer a higher level of oxygen. On Monday we will be getting a transport wheelchair (and we already have a walker, shower stool and the aforementioned portable toilet). And the weird part of it is that while I would sometimes become impatient or annoyed with the way our house seemed always to be dominated by signs of illness and infirmity—now all I can think is, "Bring it on—whatever will help—whatever will give us one more day or week or month."

Our home care nurse made her weekly visit today. With things pretty status quo for a few weeks now I found myself asking her what it would look like when we were beginning the downhill slide. She gave me some signs: Larry sleeping more, limited appetite, perhaps a lung infection of some sort. I don't know why I asked the question today except that with things seemingly more stabilized, I find myself slipping back into that old denial stage and thinking maybe he has more time.

But later a friend calls, and I hear Larry say that he is "having a rough afternoon"—evident in the way his spirits seem dampened, and his breathing seems more restricted. And because he rarely admits to anyone—even me—how he is really faring, I understand that his condition will not get better—only worse. He knows this, and underneath all the layers of denial I've put in place, so do I.

But we have today—right now, so what might I do to make that a little better for him while at the same time creating some small memory that will comfort me when he's gone?

SIX WEEKS AND COUNTING

I've been blessed to see the same therapist for several years now. He has helped me through any number of challenging times but none more challenging than the journey I am on now. In our last couple of sessions, I have talked about two things that even to say them out loud is difficult: how long will this go on and what will my future look like?

Okay, believe me I get it that this sounds incredibly self-centered. I am not the person dying here. So, to even entertain thoughts of what I might do or where I might go once this journey is over—plain talk: once Larry dies—leaves me rife with guilt that is nearly paralyzing. But as my therapist pointed out this is not about wishing for an end; it's about figuring out how I will survive once it happens. Having never been a person who lives in the moment I get that. My whole life I have operated on how I will handle whatever challenge may come along, and that entails planning past the moment. I did that when Larry first became ill eight long years ago; I did that when it became clear that our activity would be severely limited by his illness and frailty. I did that when I understood that if you get to the path you thought you would take and find the bridge out, then you find another way.

The second area of discussion—how long will this go on (with "this" being the fact of Larry's dying) is tougher. I want him here with me as long as possible, but I also respect his need for quality of life. I know his strong feelings about that. Without quality, he has no interest in quantity.

In some ways I suppose the two discussions are opposite sides of the same coin—each involves planning a life without Larry as a part of it and each involves overwhelming feelings of guilt, fear, and anxiety.

Here's the good news: Larry may be no longer physically here but as my therapist pointed out he has been such a factor in my life—more so than anyone else—that the very idea that I will go on without him is ludicrous. Through our years together we have shared so much, taught each other so much, been counselor, cheerleader and constant friend for each other and death cannot erase that. In my heart of hearts, I know that he will be with me and more to the point he is here now in every way that counts.

I just have to stop living so much in the future land of dread and worry and remember to live in the NOW. As another Jo (Muelton) once said: Life isn't about waiting for the storm to pass; it's about learning to dance in the rain!

CLOCK TICKING AS JANUARY COMES TO AN END

As we travel this road together it has occurred to me many times how truly blessed I am to be on this journey with Larry. He has been facing this destination for some time now while the rest of us—me perhaps most of all—moved along in an induced state of refusing to know or acknowledge. We were all so certain that there would come a new medicine—a cure—something to keep him going. In some cases, others still cling to that false hope. Only he acknowledges the reality.

To that end, since we came home from the hospital in December, he has been "putting his house in order." A week or so ago that involved asking me to go meet with the minister of the Unitarian church we joined years ago and find out what we need to put in place for a memorial service to come after he dies. His wish is to be cremated immediately, with a service later for friends and family which he'd rather not have but understands is not for him. Still, having accepted that, he is determined to set some ground rules:

- NO pomp and circumstance meaning no one dresses up and there is no religious overtone to the service (not that there usually is with Unitarians).
- NO maudlin eulogies—a celebration of his life rather than a dirge for his death.
- NO hymns—rather he chooses a Cole Porter song he loves titled "Experiment."
- Food from his favorite deli for the reception with a sweet table that will put every wedding or bar/bat mitzvah we've ever attended to shame.

The minister is a bit taken aback by what I am proposing. It is not what he considers the usual send-off, and for that reason he has questions. He knows me well because I have been active on several church committees and projects through the years, but he barely knows Larry. He suggests he come to the house to get better acquainted. I agree and we set a day and time.

Because he is at heart a private person, Larry is not happy with that decision. I feel things taking a downward turn when the minister arrives for the scheduled appointment—his resolute this-is-my-expression-for-serious-occasions face firmly in place. Clearly, he expects to see a man severely weakened by illness, so is somewhat taken aback when Larry greets him with a hearty, "Hi, Drew! How's it going in the religion business these days?"

The minister recovers and laughs. They chat a bit; the minister takes a couple of notes, and after maybe half an hour, Larry does what he always does when in his view an encounter is over—he thanks the man for coming and says goodbye.

January

A few days later I meet our talented music director to discuss selections for the service. Our music director is also a popular member of the local theater scene and almost always working on and/or appearing in some production. So, when I mention the Cole Porter song Larry has requested, he is delighted with the idea of being so specific.

My third task is to ask my dear friend—who played matchmaker for Larry and me years earlier—if she will handle the arrangements for the reception. She and Larry have not always been close, but when I make the request, she smiles before I can get it out. "What?" I ask.

"Larry already asked me," she replies, and is of course glad to do it.

It occurs to me that reading this, someone might think it must have been so difficult. We were, after all, planning his funeral. But the truth is one of the things I have learned over the years is that when it seems you have no control over anything, it's important to look for those things you *can* control. Larry could state his needs for what he wanted this to be, and I could make that happen.

While I have always and apparently will continue to struggle to come to terms with what I cannot control, "This is the life we get" has always been his refrain. I was slow to come on board with that philosophy, but around this time I heard about a young athlete suffering from ALS who said something like "We all have a timeline—most of us just don't live our lives that way."

Larry does.

February

Today Larry got his first tiny dose of morphine. It's meant to help increase his energy, and it did work so we were both happy about that. We joke a lot about his becoming a druggie after living a life of few—if any—vices. On the other hand, the fact that we have started down this side road is unsettling.

In a more sobering moment, our home care nurse talks about the difficulty of getting folks to understand the importance of planning for the decisions necessary as life comes to its end, reminding me that I need to start thinking about who will serve as my healthcare power of attorney and in other roles for me once Larry is gone. Of course, I had always assumed he would be the one seeing me off—not the other way round. Now he urges me to think about who will play those roles.

It is times like these when I envision a future that will be so changed as to be unrecognizable. Always someone who had next steps and new plans firmly in place to look forward to, I wonder if Larry isn't the smarter one. Aside from planning for our financial security with an obsession that sometimes drives me batty, he has always lived in the moment, only addressing what came next once the activity or project of the "now" was complete. I, on the other hand, tend to put off dealing with matters that seem to me not to need my immediate attention while focusing on plans for a future that is weeks or even a year away. It is clear to both of us that dying carries with it many decisions best made in advance, rather than the emotional heat of necessity.

I am reminded of when my father died, and the four adult children met at the funeral home to plan a service and select a casket. The funeral director was savvy enough to leave the four of us alone in the showroom where each of us continued to play our assigned family role—this one not really seeing the point of discussing something destined to be underground; another weighing costs; a third reminding us all of our father's love of beautiful wood; and me trying hard to negotiate the undercurrent of conflict that was sometimes a part of our being together. How much better might it have been had our parents met with the funeral director and made these decisions?

But I get it. When we are in our prime, death is the very last thing we want to discuss or navigate. I see now that what Larry has already put in place will prove to be a blessing when the time comes. And yet? I don't want to give into the reality of our situation. I definitely don't want to try and imagine what life will be once he's not here. And I am not yet ready to choose another candidate to entrust with life decisions for me.

It seems like just when I think I might be handling this well, I get sucker punched and find myself emotionally doubled over.

VALENTINE'S DAY

Last night I left a card I had made for Larry on the table so he would find it at breakfast. He opened it and laughed at the message then asked me to get an envelope from his desk. He is not a shopper—never has been. And while now and then I have received the store-bought hearts and flowers card, most of the time I have gotten something far more precious—a sheet of paper torn from one of the yellow legal pads he keeps on his desk with a message written in red ink and sometimes a childlike drawing to illustrate the message. On this day the message was longer than usual, and the drawing was there as well.

And, of course, as I read that precious handmade message declaring his love, it hit me that this—like so many things in our lives these days—will likely be our last Valentine's Day together. I don't mean to leave anyone with the idea that ours has been an idyllic marriage. We have certainly had our differences—and sometimes stated them with rants (me) or silence (him). There were definitely nights when we ignored the adage to never go to bed with anger between us. Still, each of us brought special traits to the marriage, and they complemented each other in ways that had us both growing as people and partners. And while I often struggled to find ways to show my love for him through gifts—a language of love I had learned as a child—he never asked for that. These days I understand I spent far too much time trying to convince myself that I was worthy of his love when it was there all the time.

If hindsight is 20/20, then I would say, looking back, we shared a love story that neither of us could have imagined when we first met and married. And once again, I think of so much precious time I wasted.

NEXT DAY–FEBRUARY

Today we sold Larry's car.

I had gone to run an errand when the new owners arrived. To my surprise, when I got home and saw the empty space in the garage, I burst into tears. Unexpected, those tears because throughout all the years of dealing with Larry's cavalcade of illness, I have rarely cried. This was a car, for heaven's sake—an old one, and yet it represented so many happy times. Drives to Florida—how we laughed as we listened to tapes of Prairie Home Companion and Mel Brooks' 2000-Year-Old Man on the old-fashioned tape deck (no CD player in this one). Trips "up North" for fishing and hiking while staying in a variety of cottages—some quaint, others funky, and one or two never-to-be-stayed-in-again but forever the source of good stories. This car got us to and from work and plays and movies and ballgames. We've always named our cars—this one was "Flash" because it was silver. Still, it is a car—a pile of metal with wheels and an engine. It could so easily be replaced. And perhaps that was the source of the tears—the realization that eventually I would have to come to terms with the absence of one who can never be replaced. And so another passage—another step down this dark road.

STILL FEBRUARY

It's the weekend and sometimes—unless I have deliberately set myself some chores and busy work—I get hit by the sweet memories of busy, fun-filled weekends in the past. The holiday gatherings we attended, the dinners we hosted, the hours of conversation with friends as we solved the world's problems. And then I remember how as recently as last fall before Larry's hospitalization, I would bitterly complain that we had no future.

Why wasn't I paying attention to the present?

I didn't get it then—I wanted the outings to ballgames and plays and movies. I thought they were important, key to who we were. I recall one specific day perhaps a year ago when I came home, exhausted by doctor appointments, and medical equipment deliveries and the sheer roller coaster we lived on, and declared, "I want our life back." Of course, what I meant were those times before—before he got sick, before the convoy of health issues descended: the stroke, the brain tumor, the ablations, the pneumonia, the pulmonary hypertension—the end game we now faced.

Now I treasure every night that Larry and I have left to spend together, talking, watching basketball or a movie on TV and bringing in take-out. I treasure the willingness of our friends to always come here instead of being able to welcome us into their homes. I repress the thoughts that come later in the night as I lie alone in our bed listening to Larry's oxygen machine pulsating life into him in the other room.

That day looms closer—the day when this journey to widowhood that still seems so surreal will have reached its destination and life as I know it now will change—in ways I have no tools for imagining or understanding.

LARRY'S BIRTHDAY

We wake knowing what this is—another last time, but attack the day determined to make it as normal as possible. Cards and calls from friends and family arrive. His sister delivers her gift in person. I bake his favorite chocolate cheesecake. Dinner is just the two of us as he wishes. We talk about our life together—something we do often now, dwelling on memories, knowing making plans is pure folly.

Earlier in the day he had asked about some memento he knows I must have stored away. While our dinner is cooking, I run upstairs to find it in an old trunk where I have always kept such things. In the process, I pull out a box I think is filled with photos and accidentally drop it. The contents go flying and there among them I see a small stack of letters. On closer examination I realize they are the letters Larry wrote to me the summer before I moved to Milwaukee. I have no memory of keeping them, yet here they are. I open one and then another, and I chuckle at the evidence I have just uncovered.

For much of our marriage the story he has told friends is that from the moment I arrived in Milwaukee, I was pressuring him to "M" me. It's true he would not use the word—*marry*. I, of course, denied this, preferring a version that revolved around the idea that getting married was the reason he had urged me to move. I now held in my hand the proof that my version of things was closer to reality. Here in his handwriting were words like "can't wait for you to be here," and "so looking forward to building a life together." You be the judge!

As we have our dinner, I choose my moment and bring up the topic. He sticks to the old story, teasing grin and twinkling eyes firmly in place. I slide a letter from its envelope and begin to read. He turns a couple of shades rosier than the after-effects one of his meds causes and grabs the letter from me. He denies that this is his handwriting or signature, then switches to professing that the words I read weren't what he meant. We are laughing the entire time and it all feels so wonderful.

This is us ... the banter, the laughter, the understanding, and always always the love.

LEAP DAY

I always associate Leap Year with election year as in a presidential election. This election year brings a second term for the current POTUS. I always wonder about that—the value of four more years considering the other side's full understanding that these will be the last years for this President. Doesn't that hogtie the ability to get anything of substance accomplished? Larry and I are both avid news junkies so following the circus that passes for political debate these days is a fascinating hobby for us both. I will sorely miss our discussions about issues, candidates, etc. and the often-heated debates that came with a moderate (him) facing off with a throwback hippie liberal (me). It's the same with sports. As has already been said, we *love* college basketball and as March Madness approaches, I try not to dwell on the fact that this will be our last chance to pick our teams and follow them. Larry will study players and coaches and season records while I make my picks based on such things as liking one mascot, coach, team color or school location over another.

So many things these days strike me as "last time" things. I would love to be wrong about that and sometimes—like now—when Larry's health seems more stable, I dare to hope. For his birthday lots of people baked goodies for him since he's always been pencil thin and loves sweets. His sister made chocolate pudding and chocolate chip cookies both from their mother's recipe and brought them over. She also brought with her a bouquet of the most gorgeous sunset-colored roses I have ever seen. Larry asked her to get them—for me. When I saw the roses and realized what he'd done I thought about all the times early in our marriage when he placed no importance on my need for these spontaneous and material tokens of his love. "So, buy flowers," he would say, his tone one of confusion that this was not an obvious solution. I could not seem to make him understand that the point was for *him* to bring me flowers now and again.

But then one day about twenty years in, I came home from work to find the kitchen sink overflowing with lilac. Lilacs are my favorite. He'd been out on his bike and had come across a bush in full bloom. Judging from the number of blossoms in our sink, he must have scalped the entire bush! Every spring after that there was a day when I came home to lilac.

Suddenly I understood these roses on a whole other level. He couldn't manage lilac because it wasn't yet spring, but he would make sure I had my surprise bouquet one last time.

March

We've switched to daylight saving time so at 5:00 a.m. it is pitch black when I wake and get up to check on Larry, making sure that the tubing for his oxygen isn't tangled or pinched. He is sleeping, the tubing is fine, and I go back to bed but not to sleep.

I lie there thinking back two to three years—recalling the almost imperceptible process of Larry's decline. There was the time when I took over all the yard work—mowing the grass, shoveling the snow, raking the leaves, trimming the bushes—things he once did with me or on his own. Back then I thought that taking on these chores was a small price to pay for giving him more time and the energy reserves to do the things he enjoyed, especially spending time biking and fishing with his friends. It never occurred to me in those earlier days that eventually that slow process of letting go of all those things would lead us to this. And although our life has fallen into a routine now that I understand will become even more restricted as the days and weeks go by, I cannot help wondering what Larry is feeling.

As the clock ticks off the pre-dawn minutes, I realize he is awake and moving around. My instinct is to go to him, but something holds me back. I sit on the side of the bed and wait, listening. He is muttering to himself and then more clearly, I hear the swears coming—the F-word he rarely utters repeated with increasing force.

And I understand that under the cover of my being in another room and the oxygen machine whirring away, he is finally taking off the mask he wears for me and others. I realize that he has thought through so much of what will come after for me. His insistence that unless there is a real need for me to be closer, I sleep in our bed rather than on the sofa next to the recliner where he sleeps takes on new meaning. I realize he is preparing me for the weeks and months and years ahead when I will likely sleep alone. I understand that he has chosen to take his feelings inside, to shelter them there rather than share them. My heart clutches with the angst and isolation he must feel.

MID-MARCH

These days I liken our situation to that of sitting at a railroad crossing—the gate is down, the lights are flashing, the warning bells are dinging, and we can see the train. But it just sits there and so do we. We know that eventually it must come but we can't say when—so we wait.

Most days are good.

Larry is still here—frail of body but healthy in mind and spirit—and that makes life bearable.

However, I will admit that there are days when I struggle against the bonds that currently hold my future prisoner. And the result of that is that I battle guilt and anger at myself and my selfish need to inwardly whine about "my life" when what Larry is facing is "no life." The domino that falls after that is my lack of patience with anyone who isn't dealing with a situation that I see as horrid as ours, bemoaning his or her lot in life. And the domino after that is my ingrained reaction to shut myself away from others—to crawl into my shell and feed on my own self-pity.

My writing room at home is upstairs in our loft area. More often than I care to admit, I go up there in the evenings, saying I have some work to do. More often than not, Larry naps after we have our dinner. More often than not, I do no work—rather I sit at my desk and stare at a computer screen, sometimes playing mindless games. And the hours go by unnoticed and wasted.

Time that could have been spent with him, even if he was sleeping.

Time I might have used to remember or to plan.

Time I cannot get back ... ever.

For several days now I have been awfully close to that need to shut myself away. But then today I went out to pick up some branches that had fallen over the winter and I saw a hint of snowbells, early spring flowers just beginning to risk breaking through the soil, and I understood that in time I too will find my way.

ENDLESS MARCH

On any given day I accomplish no more than the basics. In some ways I am surprised at the ordinariness of our life. No drama; no catastrophic events; no drop-the-mike epiphanies. Our days seem strangely normal. At Larry's urging, I go off to my studio—supposedly to work but most days I spend at least half the time staring out the window or rearranging the books and files and furniture. Every day I am at the grocery store seemingly incapable of planning ahead for more than one meal. I meet friends for coffee a couple of days a week and another hour or so slips by. After supper Larry and I settle in to watch television. At ten I go off to bed to read and he does the last round of his daily routine of stretching exercises before settling in for the night. In spite of what he has been told and knows in his heart, he continues to do everything he can to maintain strength.

The next day we get up and do it all again.

When I try to consider why I seem incapable of accomplishing more, it occurs to me that I begin and end each day in a state of waiting—will there be a change? Where will things be a month from now? Three months from now? A year from now?

MARCH 31–OUR ANNIVERSARY
Forty-two years.

Seems like yesterday.

We were married in my home state of Virginia at the historic Martha Washington Inn—a special place in Abingdon, a town that resonates with the past. As has always been our tradition, we sit together and watch the DVD I had made of our wedding photos—the photo journal Larry's best man made of their trip to Abingdon and the morning of the wedding. We laugh at the memory of how when Larry proposed I thought he was breaking up with me and how he refused to say what he referred to as the "M" word—as in Will you "M" me? He admits to having been terrified, while I felt only a sense that at long last, I had found my safe place. We smile at the photo of him with my dad—Larry looking like he's ready to bolt and Daddy with a huge smile that says, "At last—another daughter out of the house."

We were married in the morning in order to make an afternoon flight to New York for our honeymoon. My brother-in-law performed the ceremony—one of only a handful he officiated at before deciding the ministry was not for him. Larry always teased me that he was never quite sure the marriage was legal.

Our reception was a brunch, and by late-afternoon we were in New York, staying at the Waldorf Astoria and seeing a Broadway play every night. It was the perfect beginning. Back in Milwaukee after a few days, Larry's mom held a lovely party for us with all the Milwaukee relatives and our friends in attendance. Forty-two years later, we look through those photos and take stock of the years—over four decades. So many adventures—and challenges.

Where did the time go?

Larry wants to try and list all the business ventures we began—together and individually. Some failed spectacularly, but a few flourished and gave us some of the happiest memories of our life together. We were never what could be considered wealthy—more comfortably middle class, but that comfort came from his vigilance when it came to managing the finances. I didn't always agree with the choices he made, but I trusted that in this area he was the expert, and as the time approaches when I know I will be the one managing such things, I find myself quietly planning how that will happen—who I will trust for advice and counsel.

We do not talk now of a future the way we usually have on this day. We find solace in the past—in the evidence of a marriage that brought laughter and joy and yes, at times, heartache, and angst.

That night we lie together—him coming to our bed for the first time in months. He won't stay because he cannot be away from the oxygen or breathe well lying down. But we find our places—me tucked against his side, my body puzzle-linked to his, my head on his shoulder, his shallow breath caressing my hair. I squeeze my eyes shut to hold back tears. I hear him sniffle and know he is doing the same.

Too soon he eases away after kissing my forehead. He is almost to the door when he turns. "Promise me," he says softly, "that you will reach out to our friends and let them care for you."

He has spoken to me and others of his fear that I will shut myself away, go into my shell and rebuff all efforts to draw me out. He has reason to worry for over the years I have often said that once he is gone, I will leave—that the friendships are really through him and do not carry the same lifelong connection with me. It is something I have thought about often as I prepare myself for life without him.

I hesitate. Then I agree. "But I want something in return," I tell him. "I want you to let me know you are with me. I mean send me signs."

He laughs that wonderful laugh everyone so loves and for an instant, he is not a man who spends his life tethered to an oxygen machine. He is that same man who stood next to me forty-two years ago and made another promise he kept beyond anything I ever imagined.

"Just you wait," he says.

April

One of the heartwarming—and frankly amazing—experiences Larry and I have had as we've traveled this road is the way friends have stepped up to support us emotionally and in some cases by physical acts of kindness. Larry is blessed to have an entire group of friends/buddies dating back to his elementary school days. Several of them still live close enough to come and go often—weekly lunches, impromptu calls, and visits. But several live some distance away—far enough that a visit requires the expense of a flight and—since we cannot have people staying here right now—a hotel. And still they come—a mark of how they treasure time spent with this man who through their lives has been there for them in good times and bad.

One friend has called every single day since Larry was in the hospital last December, and he has made the trip to visit now twice with plans for a third visit next month. When I drove him to his hotel tonight, he indicated that he hopes to visit monthly for as long as this lasts. Amazing! But not so much if you knew Larry. He inspires this kind of loyalty through the low-key way that he places the focus always on others rather than himself. If you ask him directly about how he's doing, he might answer honestly and briefly or shrug off the question before turning the conversation back to you or other topics. He has a gift for appreciating even the seemingly insignificant moments.

I often think about how people use the phrase "after a long and courageous battle with..."—well, Larry is the poster child for that phrase. Through his refusal to allow his own anger and sadness and whatever else he has to be feeling color his relationships with others he has won for himself—and for me—this incredible safety net of support and caring that I know will continue to sustain me in the days after he is gone.

APRIL–FOUR PRECIOUS MONTHS

For us I think this stage could be called the calm before the storm. We know what's coming but we have been blessed with this time together. I often think how much worse it would have been had he died suddenly. I have been given the gift of time—time to prepare, time to remember, time to say goodbye.

As each day unfolds with only minute changes to his condition, I realize how very much I have changed (and for the better). Was it only last fall that I was walking through life with a face that screamed *poor me*? And yet these days I feel such a calm comfort in the very fact that a new day dawns and we are both still here—able to enjoy our life together, our friends and family, the things that have become our new routine. Faced with the opportunity to travel—an opportunity Larry has encouraged—I find that I am reluctant to do so. Why would I want to miss a single precious day that we might share?

I promise him I will travel ... later ... after.

MID-APRIL

I thought there would be some significant event or sign, but quietly and without fanfare last month we made the transition from palliative to hospice care. We have a new nurse calling on us every day now, and we look forward to her visits for all sorts of reasons. First, she is an interesting woman with a sense of humor that is a good match for Larry's teasing. She respects his need to hear information with no sugarcoating the facts. She has quickly become someone we both trust to honestly answer our questions and troubleshoot any problems we may be having.

This week she alerts us to the fact that we are coming to the end of the first certification period. Not sure I got all this right since basically he just switched to hospice, but apparently, she will need to show a reason why Larry should continue or be on hospice in the first place, which is laughable. It's not like he's going to suddenly make some miraculous progress.

I admit that the first thought that runs through my mind is that apparently the powers that be have set a sell-by date on how long it should take a person to die. But I do get it that—as with any system—there can be abuses. Still, it is upsetting to realize that we might lose this support that has become so important in both our lives.

There is no question that he is failing albeit by small sometimes hard to measure increments. And frankly sometimes the reason I look forward to the nurse's visit is because Larry will explain what he's experiencing in greater detail than he will admit to me or others. Today he describes how this morning while brushing his teeth, he became so weak that he wasn't sure he was going to finish before he had to sit down. She asks if he might want the return of an aide (not needed since shortly after the hospitalization in December), but he refuses. After the nurse leaves, I get out a shower stool we had in storage (there's already a built-in seat in the shower he uses) and set it against the wall just opposite the bathroom sink. That way he'll have something to sit on should this kind of weakness continue—which obviously it will. So, another small concession to this thing that is slowly killing him.

Later in the week when I leave for a dental check-up, all seems to be what passes for normal these days. Larry is at breakfast, reading his paper, phone nearby for the first calls of the day. I give him a kiss and tell him I might stop by my studio to work after the appointment. He warns me he expects to read the next chapter of the novel I am currently working on when I return. His editing of my work has been instrumental in any success I've enjoyed as a writer. After the appointment I go to my studio, lose myself in the story I am currently working on for a couple of hours, and then go grocery shopping. Throughout the day, Larry and I have checked in by phone.

When I come home, Larry is in his recliner with the TV tuned to the business channel he often watches during the day. He is napping—not usual at this time of day but also not unusual. I leave him alone as the oxygen delivery arrives. I deal with calls from friends in need of an update. And every time I check on him, he is still asleep.

Suppertime comes and goes, and he doesn't want anything. Now I am worried. I try to rouse him, but he pushes me away. The dread that comes like a switch being thrown whenever there is some signal that things are deteriorating in a more major way throws me into action. I want to call the hospice nurse. He refuses, his temper short, his body language and facial expression sending clear messages of, "Leave me alone." This, I have come to understand, translates into the fact that something is not right and he knows it.

I walk a fine line between making sure that things are the way he wants them to be and the need to make sure that I am doing all I can to keep him with me. At the same time with each day that passes and each episode that reminds me he will not be here much longer, I understand that for him, finding the will to continue fighting for one more day is becoming more difficult. He has prepared himself and has tried to prepare me. I am closer to understanding that it is selfish of me to ask him to keep pushing forward when his quality of life is pretty much non-existent.

At dinner one night a week or so ago, I said, "You are handling everything with such grace and even humor, but inside...." He looked at me for a long moment and finally said. "Inside I am so angry, I can barely contain it."

And there it was—finally. The human question of "Why me?" This is a man who has done everything right—never smoked, maintained a rigorous exercise and nutrition regimen even before such routines were commonplace, played by all the rules.

There was nothing more to say.

Another hour passes, and he finally agrees I can call hospice. Two nurses come out—check his vitals and give him morphine and something for nausea. His blood pressure is high, but his lungs are clear. They offer in-patient hospice as an option. This, I know, is his worst nightmare and when he refuses, I back him up. I am holding it in reserve, hoping to keep my promise that he will die at home.

But at the same time, I ask myself repeatedly: What is the right thing to do?

I feel as if he has taken this dramatic turn and is slipping away from me. I want to sit by him and hold him—or at least hold his hand but he doesn't want that, and again dismisses me with a look. So hard—so scary. So utterly terrifying, as somehow, we make it through the night.

May

Once again it appears we have dodged a bullet. Larry has had a spurt of energy and improvement since mid-April, although there continue to be little signs—things that might be missed if we didn't know what was coming. We went out to eat the other night—something we've been able to do at a small select group of restaurants for the last couple of months. Always before Larry has walked from the car—parked as close as possible to the entrance—into the restaurant where we've gotten a table closest to the door and enjoyed our meal. Then he walks back to the car for the drive home and then from car into house. These latter two trips can be exhausting for him even with the support of his portable oxygen tank, but he is determined.

Tonight, once we had eaten, I truly did not think he was going to make it—either to the car or into the house. His breathing was so very shallow and the effort of taking each step was clearly monumental.

Another last time.

It strikes me how many of these final events creep up on us without warning. When we left for the restaurant tonight, if we had known this would be our last time going out together, would we have chosen a different place? Denial prevents us (or perhaps just me) from admitting what is right there to see.

A WEEK LATER

Rough night tonight. After we go to bed, I hear Larry moaning and moving around. I go to him and find him desperate to transfer from his chair to portable toilet. "I have to go," he whimpers, clearly in pain. Somehow, I am able to get him to a standing position and then drag/lift him onto the toilet.

Nothing.

I repeat the lift/drag dance and get him back to his recliner for some sleep while I take up my position on the sofa.

We repeat the above every 15–20 minutes or so until I insist we call the hospice nurse. By now it is after three in the morning, and we are both beyond exhausted. He still has not been able to empty his bladder.

The agency assures me the nurse on call is on her way.

An hour passes and finally she shows up, having stopped to pick up someone else. I don't have the patience or energy to question why. She is our lifeline of the moment, and I will not endanger that. In the meantime, Larry and I have managed half a dozen more transfers to and from with no results. I step aside while she does her thing, examining him, asking him questions he is too exhausted to answer. Then turning to me, she says, "I can't help him. He needs to be admitted to in-patient hospice."

With surprising strength Larry grabs my hand to get my attention. His eyes on me, he shakes his head. And I know

May

what he was saying. *If this is it, I want it to happen here. Do this for me.*

"He's not going anywhere," I tell the nurse who I had never met and who had already made it clear she was less than empathetic to what we had endured over the last several hours.

Her eyes widen in what I see as shock that I would dare question her opinion. Immediately she packs up her things and says, "Then you're refusing help?"

"We are refusing a transfer to the hospital," I clarify, stepping between Larry and her in what has become widely known as Mama Bear stance.

Her colleague has said nothing since entering the house. The nurse turns to her and says, "Let's go."

And they leave.

I don't bother to lock the door or turn off the outside lights. Instead, I kneel by my husband of over forty years. "You're sure?" I ask, knowing all I really must do if he changes his mind is call 911.

He grips my hands and manages a single word. "Sure."

Over the next several hours we repeat the on-off routine with no results and him weaker by the minute. At that point I just do not want him dying in such misery. Just before dawn he finally falls into the deep sleep of exhaustion. I call the agency and leave word that our regular nurse should come as soon as possible.

She arrives half an hour later and immediately I see a change in Larry. He trusts this woman. Very quickly she assesses the problem. Together we move him to the bedroom, and she installs a catheter to empty the bladder—something the previous nurse could have—*should* have done. Within minutes, Larry is sleeping peacefully. She stays with us until she is certain the issue has been resolved. During this time, she suggests that I allow her to order a

The "W" Word

hospital bed for the family room as well as a larger capacity oxygen machine. I agree without asking Larry.

By noon he is better than he has been in days. He talks to friends on the phone. His sister comes to visit. A dear friend stops by. His laughter fills the house once again. The nurse leaves. I prepare a light lunch and he is actually hungry. My hope that we still have time is restored.

Later in the afternoon the home care agency arrives to deliver the equipment the nurse ordered. When he sees the bed being set up, Larry is livid. He asks the man assembling the bed to stop. The man looks at me, clearly aware there is a problem here.

By now I am running on fumes, and in no mood for this new battle of wills with my husband. I am doing what *he* wants. I would crawl over crushed glass to keep him with me one more day/hour/minute, and I have repeatedly honored his wishes and refused hospitalization. I see the bed as further proof I am accepting he will die sooner rather than later and at home. What is his problem?

From somewhere in my diminished reserves, I pull up the one answer I think might change his mind about accepting the need for the bed. "Do it for me," I say. "You don't ever have to get into that bed, but for me it will be a place of rest better than the sofa. I am not leaving you alone again."

Time stands still as the delivery man looks at Larry and waits. Finally, Larry nods, and the work continues. Once the man leaves, I do not make up the bed, hoping this will reassure Larry that the bed is not for him.

As the afternoon fades into evening, his strength also fades. The catheter has been removed and he is back in his recliner. He eats a little dinner and asks me to turn off all the lights except the TV. I also turn down the volume on the TV since he is drifting in and out of sleep. I think little of this because overall it has been a good day following a horrific night and we are both in need of sleep.

I stare at the flickering images on the TV. Not really watching, just digesting the last 24 hours—the panic, the anger, the resolve, the hope . . . all accompanied by the drumbeat of knowing that it's coming.

MAY 9–THE DAY I WILL REMEMBER THE REST OF MY LIFE

Around midnight Larry becomes restless—agitated. I switch off the TV and kneel next to him. Springing into action has become second nature to me. What does he need? Want? How can I make him more comfortable? My mind rockets into solution-mode.

His voice is barely audible, refusing everything I offer with a slight shake of his head. "Tell me what to do," I plead and lean in close to make out his response.

"I want you to get some sleep," he says.

I hesitate. Still, the hospital bed is right there, and I am so tired. Perhaps allowing him to care for me is the right thing. I lie down on the bed I never made up, pulling a throw pillow closer. I reach out and touch his arm, reassuring myself that we can still reach each other should I fall asleep. I give him the secret signal we developed years ago to say, "I love you." He struggles to return the interlocking of his index fingers—a bit of silliness he invented years ago as a way to reassure me when we were in a crowd or at a party across the room from each other. I smile and close my eyes, surrendering to the weariness that inhabits every fiber of my being.

Something wakes me, but the room is filled with silence other than the rhythmic sound of the oxygen machine in the hall. I open my eyes, adjusting to the blackness. Larry's eyes are open, and he is looking at me. I see snot dripping from his nose around the tubing that is his lifeline. I see drool that wets his chin. I get up and gently wipe his face and remember that in the kit the nurse left a few days ago, there was something meant to stop this loss of fluids. I can't recall what.

I speak to him, call his name. He does not answer.

I call the home care agency. They tell me what to do, and then quietly add, "Do you want us to come?"

I answer in the affirmative and race to get the small pads I am to put behind his ears to stem the loss of fluids. At the same time on autopilot, I open the front door, turn on outside lights before hurrying back to him. I struggle to open the package.

Why must they make it so difficult?

And then I stop. His chin rests on his chest. Gently I lift his head. His jaw is slack. I close his mouth, my fingers tracing the fullness and fading warmth of his lips.

Because I know.

Now the silence in this room is total. There are distant noises . . . traffic on a street nearby, the song of an early morning bird, even the hum of the oxygen machine is a distant murmur. In this room, there is only stillness.

Gently I remove the oxygen tubing and wipe his face with a damp cloth. I kiss his lips and stroke his unshaven cheek.

This is my husband—the love of my life—my best friend—*my* lifeline.

And he is gone. And what I had feared most has happened. I am alone.

The nurses arrive and confirm what I already know—what they no doubt expected to find. They tell me they will clean him up and change him—dying is a messy business as it turns out. I bring them clothes and they smile. No funereal suit with crisp shirt and tie for this man. Rather he will go in his favorite shorts and a T-shirt bearing the logo of his beloved alma mater. They suggest if I need to make calls to family and friends, I should go ahead with that for it will take them some time to get him ready.

I glance at the kitchen clock and see that it is nearly five a.m. I call his sister first, and once assured that she and her husband and daughter are on their way, I call the funeral home to arrange for the body to be taken to the crematorium. Then I start calling friends—those closest to him and others close to me who I know will spread the word. I call my sister in North Carolina and ask her to tell my brother and let me know once they have made plans so I can send someone to bring them from the airport.

Larry's sister and family arrive, unsure of what to do or say. I—who have never been a hugger—embrace my sister-in-law, knowing in many ways her loss is as great as mine. Her parents and only sibling are now all gone.

The nurses, carrying a large black garbage bag filled to capacity, ask if I want some time alone now that they have finished their work. I direct them to the garage to dispose of the bag and then to the kitchen to make whatever calls they need to make. I walk down the hall to the room where we have spent so much of these last few months. The nurses have dressed Larry and placed him on clean sheets on the bed he never wanted to occupy. I realize I have no idea where those sheets came from.

It is full morning now—a beautiful May Day. I sit on the side of the bed and touch his face. He is not there. This is a mannequin and the tears I had thought would come do not.

I have lived so much of my life doing what I felt I was supposed to do, feeling what I thought I was supposed to feel, saying, or thinking what I believed I was supposed to say or think. I am by nature one who seeks peace—sometimes at my own expense—and finds it easier to seek comfort for others rather than for myself. I am a person who has been burned often enough that my trust factor is quite low.

But I trusted this man. He is gone. What now?

I stand, then lean in to kiss him just in case the spirit has not completely left. Back down the hall I see the nurses are ready to leave, their work done for the time being. They tell me that later in the day people will come to dismantle the bed and remove the breathing machine and other equipment. They speak words of admiration for this man who made them laugh and who always took an interest in their lives. They tell me how special he was. They have tears in their eyes.

I see them out then suggest Larry's sister go be with him and have some time if she wants. The funeral home comes for the body. I stand and watch as they bring it out through the house and front door. They have wrapped it in a quilt I provided.

My beloved husband and partner in life has become an impersonal "it."

The funeral director tells me that per Larry's wishes once cremation takes place later this week, he will personally deliver the ashes. I thank him profusely as I did the nurses.

It's as if I cannot fathom how incredibly kind people are being—as if I don't deserve their kindness. Larry is gone and my mind races with should-have's and why-didn't-I's. And at the same time, I am amazed by my tranquility and ability to function—as are others although they will tell me later, they are certain I must have been in shock.

Soon after the body is removed, Larry's sister and family leave as well. Neighbors have stepped outside to watch the hearse leave and one or two cross the street to ask what they can do. One offers an extra refrigerator she has in her garage to hold the food she assumes will be coming. I thank her and accept and can't help mentally sending Larry a message that I have taken the first step toward fulfilling my promise. I have accepted the kind offer of my neighbor rather than my usual reaction to assure her I could manage. For the rest of the morning, I stay busy making calls and arrangements. Just after noon the home care pick-up van arrives to get the bed and oxygen machine.

I spend much of the afternoon on the phone, assuring friends I am doing all right but am really exhausted. I ask them not to come until tomorrow. For once, they hear me and do not insist. I talk to my sister and brother and learn when they will arrive. I make arrangements for them. My sister and her husband will stay with me, and I reserve a room in a nearby motel for my brother and sister-in-law. I call friends to pick them up at the airport when they arrive the following day. Somehow, I continue to force myself to do what I promised Larry I would—I ask for and accept help.

Finally, it is dark outside, and I am alone. The phone is silent for the first time all day. I walk through the rooms of the house as memories surround me. There is still much evidence of our odyssey through sickness and pain over these last months. I instinctively know that the first thing I need to do—the thing Larry would want me to do—is eradicate all evidence of that. I must restore our home to those times when his illness had not yet set up residence. I need to make this house a home again.

I work deep into the night—cleaning and tossing and rearranging. Storing medical stuff that cannot be returned (portable toilet, walker, quad-cane, etc.) out of sight in the attic storage area. I take the foot brace he had to wear after the stroke and stuff it in the garbage. I run loads of laundry and remake our bed, then make up the bed in the guest room. Finally, I rearrange furniture in the living and

The "W" Word

family rooms from a floor plan intended to accommodate medical equipment and uninterrupted traffic patterns for him to navigate to the more satisfying conversational grouping he preferred. And, just as the first light of dawn lightens the sky, I wrap myself in the fleece shirt he loved as I curl into the recliner where he spent his last hours and watch the new day arrive.

The new day that is the beginning of a new life for me....

PART TWO
The Journey THROUGH

Still May

Larry died two days ago.

Note the avoidance of any euphemism such as "passed on," "passed over" or simply "passed."

He died.

He always hated the fact that people avoided calling it what it was. He was especially annoyed when anyone described the event as "we lost Mary today." His thought was always either "Where exactly did you lose her?" or "Why aren't you out looking for her?"

The first part of this memoir is called "Journey TO Widowhood." That journey ended at 3:30 a.m. on May 9th. Larry's death and my entry into this strange new world came at the same moment. In the nearly 48 hours that have passed—48 hours that at times have seemed more like 48 seconds and at other times more like 48 weeks—I have run the gamut of emotion.

Fear, anger, weariness, relief, happiness.

The happiness part is realizing that he is no longer in a fight—no longer struggling to make it one more day. I don't know what happens in the world beyond this one, but I want to believe that Larry is finally whole again—filling his lungs with fresh air as he runs unencumbered by his stroke and bikes for miles with no problem. That image makes me smile and brings me peace. But then the reality of my own future darkens my spirits to a level of overwhelming angst and sadness. I will have to find new ways to do almost everything.

I have started to keep a mental list of "first times"—first time I asked waiter for separate checks for me alone when I agreed to go out for dinner last night; first time I signed my sister-in-law's birthday card with only my name not Larry's; first time I went out and returned to an empty house. First times that add to the litany of last times. First times to be replicated many times over the coming months and years until they become new habits and routines.

Today he was cremated, and tomorrow there will be a memorial service—one that we planned together. I am surrounded by family and friends, their calls and visits sustaining me in these early hours and days, and yet. . . .

Two days in. What will four be like? Fourteen? Forty? Four hundred? My friend whose husband died a few years ago tells me the second year is the hardest. How can anything possibly be harder than this?

MEMORIAL SERVICE

The day begins. I have done what I can for Larry, his family, our friends, and still there are those who are disappointed with decisions I have had to make on the fly and in the throes of my disbelief that I have reached this moment in my life. For the first time in over forty years, Larry is not here to stand with me, to be a buffer to the demands and wishes of others.

I take the families—his and mine—out for lunch. We share stories about him, smiling at the memories. Neither family is the crying sort, although I can see they are concerned that I am not more tearful. We walk back to the church, which is full. We wait in the reception hall until the minister arrives to escort the family into the sanctuary. We walk single file behind the minister and take our places in the front pew. I can feel eyes on me the way those attending might focus on the bride at a wedding. They want to see how I'm holding up, I suppose. I glance around, and I see that everyone has respected Larry's wishes—they are dressed casually as if going to a basketball game or night at the movies. So far, so good, I think and feel the tension that has gripped me all morning ease a bit.

The music director is playing a lively Broadway tune and I see that he has brought along a woman he often performs with to further enrich the service. His kindness touches me, and we exchange a smile. On the dais sit the minister and four of Larry's friends. They will speak once the minister has made opening remarks. They are under strict orders that whatever they do, they must be upbeat. I appreciate how difficult that may be for them. After all, this man was their lifelong friend, and they are also grieving.

The minister rises and his remarks are largely based on information I gave him in that first meeting in his office. He does not know Larry well and admits that openly, but acknowledges the tribute being paid to him by the presence of so many. The music director and his friend sing a duet—again, a show tune—and then the first of the four friends takes the microphone. Soon the sanctuary is filled with laughter—these men are all lifelong friends who knew Larry so well. They do not sugarcoat his idiosyncrasies and even those in attendance who are there more for me than because they knew him are soon caught up in the spirit of the moment. It is exactly what Larry wanted, and I realize that for the first time in days I am not just smiling—I am laughing along with everyone else.

The tributes (for they can hardly be called eulogies) end and the music director takes his place at the piano. He looks at me and smiles, then plays the opening chords of the song Larry requested, and sings:

> Before you leave these portals
> To meet less fortunate mortals,
> There's just one final message
> I would give to you.
> You all have learned reliance
> On the sacred teachings of science,
> So I hope, through life, you never will decline
> In spite of philistine Defiance
> To do what all good scientists do.
> Experiment.
> Make it your motto day and night.
> Experiment
> And it will lead you to the light.
> The apple on the top of the tree
> Is never too high to achieve,
> So take an example from Eve,
> Experiment.
> Be curious,
> Though interfering friends may frown.
> Get furious
> At each attempt to hold you down.
> If this advice you always employ

> The future can offer you infinite joy
> And merriment,
> Experiment
> And you'll see.
>
> Cole Porter, 1930

And in that moment, I understand. He chose this song for me. The words are directed at me. Once again, he is giving me my marching orders—the way forward.

Experiment.

There is a hush as the final note floats away, then the minister asks everyone to stand while the family leaves. I am thankful there is a side exit at the front of the sanctuary, so we don't have to make a trip up the aisle, passing people along the way. I need a moment—a moment I don't really get, for as soon as we reach the hallway, it's time for my brother and sister-in-law to take the ride I have waiting for them to the airport. They must be at work first thing tomorrow and have a long day of travel to navigate. I am so grateful they came.

Through the closed door of the sanctuary, I can hear the minister announcing that the family will gather later in the evening, and he gives the address of our home. I head into the reception hall, now fully laid out with a spread of food from the deli and enough home baked desserts provided by our friends to feed a small country. Someone suggests a place for me to stand and receive people. I invite Larry's sister to stand with me, but she declines, and so I wait alone.

As I mentioned earlier, I am not a hugger in the sense of every time I see someone I know we exchange a hug and perhaps an air kiss. I don't get that. For me, it takes away the specialness of the hug. And what about being expected to hug someone you'd rather not for whatever reason? Does some silly social protocol demand obedience?

But I digress, and on this day, I also diverge from my usual resistance.

On this afternoon, I give and receive more hugs than I have probably shared with other than Larry in my lifetime. Some approach me with caution and sad expressions. Others are more direct readily enfolding me in their arms and offering the warmth of our shared grief. If ever there was a special moment when a hug was the best possible medicine for both the giver and recipient, this is it. I know Larry is pleased. All around me the atmosphere in the hall continues to be festive. There are people who have come that I have not expected. There are people who have come just for me. I know that because the only way they know Larry is through me. And there are those people who have been there for all the joys and challenges of our life together—our friends, as dear to both of us as family. The minister tells me in all his years he has never been part of an end-of-life celebration like this one.

By the time I give and receive the final hug, all around me people are talking and eating and laughing. I have arranged for a microphone to be set up in case there are those who did not get to speak during the service who want to say something or share a memory. A few do just that and when they are done, I thank everyone for coming and invite them again to join us at the house later. I am surprised but grateful for my poise as I lapse into "hostess" mode. I can see others breathing a sigh of relief as well.

From somewhere in my sub-conscious, I hear Larry say, "You throw a hell of a party, lady!" It is what he always told me as we lay in bed after entertaining a houseful of guests. Remembering that brings such calm and comfort.

As others leave, my friends and I pack up the leftover food—plenty for the evening ahead and tomorrow evening as well. I look forward to those times, knowing that once again the house will be filled with the activity we so often enjoyed over the years. I am grateful the other women do not try and stop me from helping with the clean-up. They know from experience that after any party Larry and I hosted, I never allowed others to clear or do dishes. I finally was able to convince them that I savored those hours after they left, and Larry went to bed, using that time to relive the evening as I put the house in order. At the same time, I now welcome their help as we pack up the leftovers. We work in tandem, silently understanding the desire to respect what each of us may need in this moment.

My sister and brother-in-law and I head home. They will stay tonight and leave for North Carolina tomorrow. I put off thinking what the house will be like once they are gone. We unload the food, store some in the neighbor's garage refrigerator, and set up the dining room for later. My sister wants me to rest, but I am far too wired for that. I have them help bring folding chairs from the basement and set up the makings for coffee and other beverages.

Late in the afternoon I hit a wall and know I need some alone time before everyone arrives. Reluctant to "fall apart" even behind the closed door of my bedroom and definitely not in front of a loving family, I set off on a walk. We live in a suburban condo community and behind our property is a nature preserve that few people seem to frequent. I head there.

As I walk the narrow path deeper into stands of trees—a few fully in leaf, others not yet ready—I feel the pressure of my grief push against the wall of my chest, probing for chinks to break through.

Eventually the canopy of trees opens to a large field of tall grasses—grasses that had not been cut the previous fall. I can hear no traffic, no other people—only the call of birds as they find their shelter for the night.

I sit on a rough wooden bench and close my eyes. The first tears I have shed since the night he died come silently, a brook thawing in the spring. Steadily the dam breaks and I move from silent tears to audible sobs. As usual I have no tissues. I wipe my nose on my sleeve like a ten-year-old. I refuse to wipe away the tears that wet my cheeks and drip onto my blouse.

I am angry.

I am lost.

I am terrified.

I am sure I cannot do this.

But I have promised I will try.

The sobs peter out to hiccups and eventually the ridiculous sound of that makes me hear his laughter, triggering a slight smile as I gather myself and start for home. After all, he also made a promise—the promise to be here with me—to let me know he is here in whatever way he can.

Might the hiccups be the first of many signs to come?

MAY–A FEW DAYS LATER

If there is anything I know for sure, it is that dealing with facing the final months of Larry's life was a walk in the park compared to facing a single day without him.

The house seems suddenly far too big with rooms filled with furnishings and stuff I do not use. The "firsts" continue as I sort through clothing and drawers and papers. Today I found the math exercises that Larry did after he had his brain tumor removed. That was a definite case of the cure perhaps being worse than the condition. Post-surgery, he had lost so much—his writing was childlike, and he could not remember all the alphabet or count sequentially to ten. One of his great joys had been tutoring math in a GED program for adults. Once he realized he could barely recall the sum of two plus two, his spirits plummeted. He was depressed and angry. But as he did with everything else, he kept practicing until it mostly came back, and over time he reverted to his calm, "it is what it is" and "let's talk about something else" self.

The one thing that was a surprise came when we traveled to New York a year after that surgery and went to the Museum of Modern Art. Throughout our married life Larry's taste in art had been firmly rooted in reality—land and seascapes, clear depictions of some aspect of life. But on that tour, he suddenly became enamored of the abstract and splashes of color. It was hardly our first tour of MOMA, but for Larry it was a new world.

Now I am the one living in a new world. The memorial service was amazing and truly a celebration of Larry's life. I replay it in my mind, seeing it through his eyes. The upbeat music; the tributes from his friends—some sweet, some funny and one a song—how that friend held it together to sing is beyond me! The reception featured all his favorite foods. The cards and homages continue to arrive. Among those who attended the service were people I worked with years ago as well as friends of friends who Larry touched with his gentle attention to every individual. Especially touching was the presence of the children of our friends—grown now but mourning their "Uncle."

As I wander from room to room, I remember other times—happier times. Although Larry had no interest in attending class reunions, when his high school 50th came along a couple of years ago, he decided he wanted to go. Knowing he would see friends from those days he had not been in touch with for years,

I suggested perhaps we host a brunch the following day—not for the entire class, but those out-of-town and out-of-touch friends he wanted to spend more time with—maybe for the last time. I made up slips of paper with our address and the time for him to give to anyone he wanted to invite. I ordered food—too much I thought at the time but understood it could always be given away or put in the freezer. The reunion was on a Saturday night, and it was there I realized my husband—this quiet unassuming man—had been something of a rock star in high school, at least to a small close-knit group of friends. The following morning our house was filled with seldom seen classmates happy to reconnect on this more intimate scale.

I stood back and watched Larry as he relived old times with these friends—mostly men—he had once played childhood games with before they all went their separate ways. The stories came pouring forth along with the laughter. It was a magical day.

And then there was our 40th wedding anniversary—another example of Larry knowing what was coming (and that the chances of us making it to a fiftieth or perhaps even a forty-first were questionable at best). Whenever we gave a party, he pretty much left everything to me as far as arrangements and food and such, but this time, he was hands-on all the way. We were in Sarasota and he found a small restaurant, making arrangements for us to take it over for the occasion. We invited all our Sarasota friends as well as friends from Milwaukee and other places. Some came; others sent their regrets and best wishes. We decorated the tables with seashells and balloons—a tribute to our admiration for Marquette University's legendary basketball coach Al McGuire. Everyone had prepared a toast—some funny, others more serious. The food was delicious, and the owners of the restaurant went out of their way to make everything perfect.

Forty years. All of them filled to the brim. The business ventures we tried—the trips we took—the homes we delighted in—the friends. So many wonderful friends. And yes, the dark days—far fewer than the sunny ones—but there to remind us to appreciate the brighter days and moments.

These are, of course, dark days. Somehow it seems especially appropriate that after two days of blue skies and sunshine, it is a stormy night with thunder and blustery winds. The out-of-town company has departed; the friends call to check in, but already I understand they will move on with their lives—their families.

Alone. The lyrics of a Stephen Sondheim song haunt me:
. . . alone is alone—not alive.

A WEEK LATER

Today I went back to the studio I use for writing and surprised myself by actually accomplishing some decent work on a new novel I'm finishing. I probably shouldn't be that shocked since all through Larry's illness I found refuge in work. I guess I thought it would be harder to get back to it. I guess I thought it *should* be harder—that it shouldn't be so easy to lose myself in that world of fictional characters and their lives. But perhaps the truth is that when I am writing fiction, I am in control. As the line from the musical Hamilton goes, I get to decide *who lives, who dies, who tells [their] story*. And as a wise friend who has been through this has warned me: There are no should's—no rules and definitely no GPS for navigating this.

Another first: today was my first post-Larry session with the therapist I've been seeing throughout this journey—and long before. He gave me the comfort of helping me to understand how Larry's final deterioration could have come so quickly and helped me appreciate that I had kept my promise to keep him at home and be at his side when the end came.

But I have such regrets. Instead of racing around like a crazy person in that final hour, trying to find something—anything—to change the course of the inevitable, why didn't I understand? Why didn't I sit quietly, holding his hand as he slipped away—making sure the last thing he knew was my touch and voice telling him how much I loved him?

My "shrink's" words are small comfort in the greater scheme of things. Still, I am thankful that long ago I opened my mind to the value of talk therapy. I am not a support group person although I appreciate the value of that avenue for many. Despite years of being active in various organizations and activities, I am a loner. I don't do groups well—at least when it comes to my personal life. But in these times of not only dealing with my grief, but also figuring out how to rebuild a life without Larry, I appreciate that the wisdom and counsel of professional therapists of the mind is every bit as important as maintaining a healthy body.

TWO WEEKS IN

Being alone in the house is strange and yet far more comforting than I would have thought, even given my preference for being on my own rather than surrounded by well-meaning others. Larry's presence is still very much here, and I can practically hear/see/feel him raising an eyebrow when I opt to open windows rather than turn on the air conditioner as one of those unexpected summery May days comes. I talk out loud to him as I move through the rooms, reporting in on what new task I've taken care of and crossed off the list of things he left for me to manage. I have not yet called for the insulation to be added in the attic—something he was so adamant about being necessary that he wanted them to come while he was here—like breathing that dust would be okay while my opening the patio door on a nice day was practically sacrilege. I did talk him out of having the work done by promising that I would see to it after he died.

The cards and notes and donations continue—although they have slowed to enough of a trickle that I am finally feeling I can keep up with the thank you notes. Friends and family continue to check in. I went forward with a small dinner party on Wednesday night that had been planned before Larry died. I thought it might feel odd but not so. It was a lovely evening of good food and laughter and conversation among old friends.

His fishing buddies took some ashes to the pond last night and then called afterwards to tell me all about it—they scattered them at the spot where Larry thought the fishing was best. Two other friends will scatter some ashes on the bike trail as well. Then I plan to go to Madison at some point and leave some ashes along the lake path. His sister and I will scatter some in Lake Michigan. These were the places he loved—places where he was especially happy. We used to joke that my duties in tending his remains would be far easier than his might be for me if the shoe were on the other foot. I want ashes in Times Square; in the hills surrounding the Virginia town where I grew up; on the beaches of the Gulf of Mexico; in Chicago where Larry and I fell in love, as well as. . . .

Oh, how we laughed about the trip he would need to make.

The truth is that the remaining ashes will sit in a handmade box, waiting for mine to be mixed in and scattered together.

Other than the breakdown the evening after the memorial service, I have not cried much at all and, since I have been known to cry while watching a TV commercial, I find that surprising—disturbing even. Today I get in the car, a list of errands on the passenger seat. As I drive, I realize it had been weeks since I have filled the car with music. I punch the CD player button knowing the Mandy Patinkin version of the Cole Porter song is loaded.

But to my surprise, a radio program Larry loved on NPR comes on. I am so surprised I pull to the side of the road. I know I pressed the CD button which is not even close to the FM button. And then I realize what's happening. I look over at the passenger seat, half expecting to see him grinning mischievously at me. My eyes brim with unshed tears. I laugh until the tears come in earnest.

MAY–THE LONGEST MONTH

Starting over is really nothing new to me. Larry and I did it numerous times over the span of our life together. I did it several times before I even met him. So, new beginnings are pretty much what I do. Of course, for the last many years I have had someone starting over with me. Larry and I worked through the details and the questions of what we would keep and what we would let go of (physically and emotionally) as we began each phase of our life together. Early on in our marriage much of the starting over revolved around jobs and business ideas that one or the other of us wanted to pursue. Way early in our marriage the starting over was the very tough period when we tried and failed to have children, tried and failed to adopt, and came at last to the really hard decision that even one child was not to be part of our life together. He spent a lot of years working overtime to try and convince me that this was not the end of the world as I knew it . . . or wanted it to be.

My therapist recently reminded me that many people would see the need to abandon favorite activities as "giving up" while Larry looked upon those necessary moments as "letting go." His way implies a conscious rather than forced decision, and I am trying my best to follow his lead as I realize this is something we practiced together.

Certainly, when going to and from Florida became our only major travel, we let go of the idea of trips to other places, like NYC, Arizona, Europe, Canada. I still did some traveling for my work or to care for family members in Virginia but basically, other than trips to places within the state of Wisconsin, we became snowbirds. During this time Larry continued to exercise and bike and fish but those things also gradually went away. He continued to cook three nights a week but then we started eating out more and almost without my noticing his cooking days came to an end.

When he came home from the hospital last December a whole new form of starting over began—it too involved poignant episodes of letting go—realizing the likelihood that we were celebrating our last Christmas and New Year's together. Realizing that his sleeping sitting up in his recliner foretold an end to our sharing the same bed—to our being curled together spoon-fashion as we fell asleep. The list is a long one and yet we did what we needed to do and found our way to a place where every day was a gift.

And now he is gone, and I am starting over yet again—this time alone. I am out of practice with doing this on my own. I talk to Larry all the time, but the problem is that he doesn't answer. He always was a good listener, but I need more than listening.

I need him.

June

Tomorrow will mark one month since Larry died. In so many ways it seems like much much longer—in other ways it seems like he is still in the next room. I suspect I will have that same realization often over the coming months and years—that it will always strike me as a surprise.

The process continues. In the absence of family nearby, friends are everything. As I mentioned earlier, because he knew me so well one of the things Larry most feared was that once he died, I would crawl into my shell and push people away. I promised him I would not do that, and so far, I have kept that promise. I have answered/returned every phone call and accepted every invitation even when sometimes I just want to be by myself. And, in spite of my thinking that I would prefer solitude, I find that at the very least talking to and being with others helps to pass the interminable hours—especially in the evenings when I miss Larry most. At the very least, I can see the possibility that the world just might settle into some kind of new normal in time. That said, I remain a person who struggles to understand the ground rules for making such connections last. Over the course of my life, I have been blind-sided when relationships that I thought were operating on an unshakeable foundation suddenly faltered. In every case it seemed something I had done (or not done) had been the trigger. In every case, I never saw the break coming. And in every case, I had no clue how to repair the damage I had apparently done. On top of that is my penchant for low self-esteem, so that when others seek a connection, my underlying thought is, "Why?" That lifelong habit of debating what, if anything, I might bring to the table continues to be a stumbling block. But I am working on it. I am learning that for others, I wasn't just Larry's wife. I was always unique and interesting on my own.

And "on my own" is, of course, where I find myself these days.

I wake up some mornings and for a split second I forget. Larry slept in the family room for months, so being alone in bed is not new and some days I simply have the instant where I forget that he's not just down the hall. It doesn't last, but is in its way, a blessing providing me with the time I need to face whatever this new day without him will bring. A friend sent me a birthday card several years ago with the message to *Be the kind of woman that when your feet hit the floor each morning, the devil says, "Oh crap, she's up."*

I know how Larry would love that this has become my mantra. Most days it works.

STILL JUNE

As a writer I get to escape to other worlds and take on the lives of characters I create and make their lives turn out the way I want. It helps that I have deadlines to meet so procrastination is not an option. I do find it more difficult to keep writing the light-hearted romantic stories I've written for years now. Understandably, I am not feeling all that romantic these days, and frankly love stories—especially stories about a new love—are not something I find appealing. Unfortunately for me, publishing is as much a bottom-line business as any other enterprise. And for now, what the editors seek from me for that bottom-line is more of the same. But I have never played precisely by the rules, and I do work hard to insert at least a second level of depth into a predictable story. The tough part is that Larry used to read all my stories—and he was a no-nonsense editor. If something didn't make sense or appeared to be resolved too easily, he would call me on it. On the other hand, when he read a section that rang true, I would hear him say, "Damn, she's good!" These days every once in a while, when a day of writing goes especially well, I will echo that and smile.

Grief is a process—one each person must go through in their own time and at their own pace. My grief is not someone else's even though that person's best friend and true love has also died. We may be able to walk the path side by side in companionship, but I cannot be in their shoes, and they cannot be in mine. What I am beginning to learn is that I have little patience with well-meant advice, especially from those who may have grieved the loss of a parent or sibling, but never a spouse or significant other. It's a completely different dynamic—as I am sure trying to offer advice from me to a parent mourning the loss of a child would be. Of course, my growing impatience with well-intended advice is not new to this situation. I have always sought to find my own way. I am sure that goes all the way back to childhood when my sister (two years older) and I made our way through elementary and high school in the small town where we grew up. We often shared the same teachers, and I quickly learned there was some expectation that

The "W" Word

I would follow in my sister's shadow, even though we were so different. She favored math/science while I was more into history. Her homework was planned; mine last minute. I spent way too much time trying to prove I was not my sister and that I would chart my own course.

I guess that stuck because all through college and early adulthood, at jobs and within social organizations, I chafed under any hint of a one-size-fits-all world. And although I am grateful for the experience and wisdom of those who have gone before, carving my own path through grief is no different.

As a friend warned, some people I thought would be there for me are not, and others, with whom I had a casual friendship at best, have stepped up big time. I cannot judge those who disappoint me because I am painfully aware that there have been times when that shoe was on my foot, and I failed to do my part. Of course, the fact that I have become aware of this shift with barely a month passed is discouraging. I am aware of friends going out to eat or for some event that would naturally have included Larry and me, but now does not include just me. I tell myself the lack of an invitation is not deliberate or intentional. I examine my actions for any evidence that I've sent the unspoken message that I'm not yet ready. And always, I hear Larry telling me I will need to reach out. On a more positive note, I have been pleasantly surprised and frankly touched at calls and e-mails received from several people I had considered more acquaintances—people I had never expected to hear from after seeing them during the memorial. I am determined to focus on what *is* rather than what I thought would be. And I am equally determined to continue my quest to reach out to others, understanding that as time passes, they will settle into old routines that may or may not include me.

June

One of the lessons my mother drummed into her children was the value of being able to manage on your own—to entertain yourself and fill the hours when no one was around. I took that lesson to heart and was enormously disappointed when, after my father died, she shut herself away, basically waiting for others to come to her rather than finding ways to rebuild her life. Now I fully appreciate how difficult that rebuilding can be—how hard it is to be the one reaching out and making the plans and calls. Now I understand.

Some days are better than others and tears do not necessarily come when I need them most. Tears are indeed cleansing and without them, the tendency is to stuff everything inside until it feels as if I just might implode. Oddly, I can't seem to bring forth the tears when I think of Larry or how much I miss him. Instead, I sob uncontrollably at some television show or the end of a novel. Traditions and activities we shared can bring on the waterworks, or at the very least a lump in my throat. Then there is the anger—the rage that this man who was so careful, so active, so religious about his health is now gone. How is that fair? Why him and not me who regularly breaks the rules?

But as Larry would remind me, nothing about life is fair—it is what it is, and to him that always meant take every chance you have to live in the moment.

A RETREAT

Not that there's a chance in hell I will truly "heal" during this week—but I had always told Larry and everyone else that once he died, I would go off on my own for a while. The reactions to this were mixed to say the least. Larry was in full support of the idea because he knew me and how I operate.

Others were stunned.

The "W" Word

"A whole week?"

"By yourself?"

Clearly in their minds, this was a bad idea and one I would regret.

Others were "helpful."

"Maybe I could come with you."

"You should call ____ as long as you're there—have lunch, see a movie."

Thank you, but no.

I had always told Larry that if the timing was right, I would return to Nantucket where I spent several days alone one autumn researching a novel. But it is June—the start of high season on the island so it is not a good choice. New York came to mind for both Larry and me because he knew how I love it there. But I will be going to NYC later this summer for a writing conference, and perhaps that will be phase two of this whole healing thing.

In the end I settled on Madison. I woke up one morning thinking about a writers' seminar I had always wanted to attend, but never had the time. I knew the sessions filled up fast, and I was a latecomer to the party. But I decided that if there was a spot for me plus a room at my favorite place to stay on the University of Wisconsin campus it was meant to be.

The answer was YES to both and here I am.

I arrived late this afternoon, got settled in and then took a walk on State Street—the street that runs between the university and the state capitol building. Our favorite restaurant has closed and that makes me a little sad as I recall the times Larry and I sat at a little bistro table on the sidewalk eating our lunch or supper and enjoying the passing parade on the pedestrian/bike only street. I check out the performing arts center half hoping for a play because we always saw a performance of some type when we were there, but nothing is scheduled. There are other theatres, and I will look them up online. I stop at a shop that does astrological readings and schedule a tarot reading for Thursday—more on that later in the week. After returning to the hotel to drop off some stuff, I head for supper at the Memorial Union—a campus landmark with a large terrace overlooking beautiful Lake Mendota.

Inside, the Rathskeller has changed for the better—instead of mostly pre-packaged salads and sandwiches, they now have a limited but made on-site menu. You order, get a pager, and pick up your food when the pager beeps—fresher food and much more efficient! I find a place on the terrace with a relaxing view of the lake. It is hot and humid but no bugs and eventually there's a breeze. I make some calls—reassuring friends and family that I am fine, then do some prep work for the start of the workshop tomorrow. Being in the heart of dairyland, the university makes its own ice cream, so I top off the evening with a dish of chocolate peanut butter (Larry's favorite) before walking back to my hotel.

A word about the "hotel": it was once a dormitory and is now lodging for guests coming to the university for conferences, weddings, reunions, and such. The rooms are comfortable, the hallways are quiet and there's a fabulous breakfast included (plus an indoor swimming pool for those interested). Most rooms come with a view of some sort—the capitol building in the distance or the lake, and the price is reasonable. Best of all, it is in the heart of the campus, making it easy to feel the years fall away and nourish a lost youth. As I get ready for bed, all I want to do is to call Larry and tell him all that I have seen and done today as I did any time I traveled without him.

And that is the hardest part of any day. There always comes that moment when I must face all over again the fact that he is not here ... that I cannot call ... that while I have friends who are incredible and a family that is there for me, I do not have *him*. Was coming here a mistake? Not sure. All I know right now is that everything about this is much harder than I thought it would be....

JUNE-MADISON-MONDAY
Ninety+ degrees but that's Madison in summer, although it does seem early in the season for those high numbers. The workshop begins, and I turn my attention to writing. Last night while looking over the agenda for the week, I began to fear that the workshop would require more of the time I have here than I wanted. Now I understand that indeed it will be a welcome respite from processing my grief. I will learn something as I always do at these things. No one is requiring me to attend every session—I can map out the time in ways that work best for me. I will make some new connections—not likely to be lifelong, but no less engaging. I will go home with new ideas and new ways of looking at the craft of writing. For several hours a day I will be distracted from the crushing loneliness that is life without Larry.

I spend the afternoon doing research for my current novel at the Historical Society's library. I love this place—walking up a flight of stairs that a gazillion people have climbed over more than a century. The marble stair treads have taken on the shape of that foot traffic—dipping closer to the thick stone handrail where most people would choose to walk. I love the stacks—musty and filled with shelves so tightly packed that they almost bulge in places. And the reading room that has been restored to its former glory, but with the modern conveniences of computers and good lighting and such. I spend three hours there. It feels more like twenty minutes.

Afterwards I take a walk and then park myself in a chair on the terrace for an hour—lovely way to end the day. But the day is not yet over—I still need to get some reading done for class and some writing done for me.

So where does the grief therapy fit into all of this? Or do I simply let it come naturally—in moments of recognition and remembrance?

Of course, the desire to call Larry continues. We would talk several times during the day even when I was just away from the house at my studio, and when I traveled, I would always call to say goodnight at the end of it. I have thought about calling the house and leaving a voicemail as I would have if he hadn't answered, but I've already developed a habit of talking out loud to him each night before I go to sleep and that seems to be working.

I will not pretend that this isn't hard, but we had so many good memories here. Perhaps there is healing in reliving those.

JUNE-MADISON-TUESDAY

Another 90+ degree day. Larry would have to stay in with the AC running because he wouldn't be able to breathe in the heat and humidity. I like to think that now he's breathing free and doing all the stuff he loved and had to let go of as his health deteriorated. (By the way, I do get it that he's no longer breathing period but that spirit—his wonderful courageous indomitable spirit—*that* cannot be shut down!)

Class today is good—everybody feeling more open and connected, ready to share and trust. I didn't sleep much last night for some reason—went to bed at 1:30 and woke up for good at 4:00. The others critique work I submitted pre-conference, and I get some valuable feedback and insights into how others are reading the story. I always appreciate the way readers see or relate to my characters and story. It inspires me to keep going. It also shows me those weak spots where I haven't given enough information to have the scene make sense.

Afterwards I walk over to the Chasen Art Museum and see a remarkable glass exhibit. There is something about glass that always moves me—something about the play of light on transparency. In another gallery, there are some colorful abstract paintings and sculptures that Larry would have loved.

I did not visit the Terrace today. Instead, I ordered takeout and ate in my room. Somehow, I have the sense that Larry is leading me to work while I am in this place with little else to do. I am looking forward to Thursday when it's supposed to cool off, and I will take longer walks along the lake path and over to the gardens we always loved.

The adventure continues and I can really feel Larry here. My therapist was right in reminding me that "grief travels" but the good news seems to be that so does that comforting spirit.

JUNE-MADISON-WEDNESDAY
Couple of things come to mind today...

First, I realize that one of the attractions of Madison for Larry and me has always been the energy. The campus, even in the quieter days of summer, throbs with activity and life. There is a feeling of new beginnings as I sit on the Terrace at the Union and watch young people in their prime living out what might be some of the best days of their lives. I want to tell them to look for the joy, to be cognizant of the memories they are building. Sometimes I see younger kids—even toddlers—and think about someday when they are old enough to come to school here and build those memories and friendships that they will carry with them all their lives—that will in so many ways shape that future. And I know when I go to the farmer's market that sets up around the state capitol building on Saturdays there will be a different kind of energy. At either end of State Street there is this wonderful intermingling of the diversity of humanity—ages, ethnic groups, gender—as well as a kind of feeling that it is possible to open new doors—even to start over.

And that brings me to the second observation—it has been a week of new beginnings in many ways. There is no denying that things have shifted to an entirely new—and often confusing or frustrating—plateau, but there are possibilities as Larry always reminded me there would be.

Before I did not want "new"—I wanted him and our life. Now I have no choice—or perhaps I do—I can choose to embrace the idea of possibility or not.

JUNE-MADISON-THURSDAY

Some lovely surprises today—surprise #1: last night when I was reading a classmate's comments on my work, I saw a note offering to serve as a reader for the manuscript. Knowing I can no longer depend on edits from Larry and because I respect her comments and knowledge, I decide to take her up on it. I regularly employ readers to vet the accuracy and flow of my novels. We run into each other at breakfast and make the deal.

Surprise #2 came in a kind of back-handed way: I find comfort in getting a tarot card reading from time to time and had added it to my list of what I wanted to accomplish during this week. So, when I went to the shop where I had had a really great experience a year or so ago, I was disappointed to sit down with someone who not only didn't read tarot but seemed to be intent on offering me advice rather than giving me insight into the psychic world around me. It was, of course, as much my fault as hers but I left there upset and disappointed. My feelings were out of proportion to the significance of this one thing. I returned to my room. The disappointment festered. Finally, I decided to look online to see if maybe there was another venue for readings.

The "W" Word

What popped up was another reader—nearby. The woman is an artist of some repute in the area, and I liked her photo and her blog and her work. So, I called her, and we have an appointment for Saturday morning. It occurs to me that it is somehow fitting that this will be the last thing I do before leaving my Madison retreat and bringing this week to a close.

Surprise #3 is the biggie and comes when I decide to take a walk along the lake path and look for the spot where I want to scatter Larry's ashes tomorrow. At first, I have no luck and decide to take a break, sitting on a bench that overlooks the lake. Out of nowhere there is this guy—older than a student would be—who walks past me and climbs over a barrier to get closer to the lake for fishing.

Larry loved fishing and we shared many wonderful hours on lakes "up North" practicing catch-and-release.

Is he telling me something? I think maybe so. I talk to the man, asking if this is a good spot for catching. He smiles and indicates that a little further back the way I had come is an even better spot. Before taking that break on the bench, I had looked at any number of places where people had made paths down to the shore, but they had all seemed too steep and overgrown for me to navigate. Still, following his direction, I retrace my steps and sure enough not ten yards away there is a path that is neither steep nor terribly overgrown—it is perfect. I hurry back to thank the fisherman, but he is gone. I had only just left him a couple of minutes earlier. Where could he have gone? I look up and down the wide path—the wide *deserted* path. The theme from the old TV show Twilight Zone plays in my brain as I memorize the coordinates of the spot so I can return tomorrow with the ashes.

Finally surprise #4 comes when I return to my room and find a lovely note from a fellow writer I have met this week reaching out to say: Can we have coffee and stay in touch? Now *that* is Larry at work! Continuing to bring people into my life from all sorts of directions—people who will ease the way for me with their friendship. New friendships to supplement the established ones. All I need to do is be open to the possibility.

As I said to our minister when we were planning Larry's memorial: this is not *A* love story; this is *the* love story—one that continues to sustain and comfort me even as I struggle with every new day.

JUNE-MADISON-FRIDAY

Yesterday was a full day—last day of sessions for the workshop plus all those surprises, and I fell into bed, exhausted. Today promises to be an emotional day that begins at sunrise with taking Larry's ashes to the spot I found. On the way—practically outside the door of where I'm staying, I find this black feather. Somehow feathers have been symbols in this journey going back eight long years to the eagle feather that Larry found on that Maine beach the day before his stroke. So, I pick up the feather and walk along the lakeshore. Again, the path is deserted.

I easily find the spot—how had I missed it yesterday? I climb down to the shore where I gather some small rocks lying there. One of them has a flat surface and all of them are this wonderful reddish color. I had brought along a marker, so I write Larry's name and Class of ___ and his birth/death dates on the rock. I sprinkle half the ashes on the ground and stack the rocks. I finish it off by placing the feather with the rocks. Then I walk to the spot where I saw the fisherman last night and scatter the rest of the small packet of ashes I brought on the water lapping at the shore.

Once again, I sit on the bench to look out at the lake and just think about Larry. It is a perfect day, huge fluffy clouds against a brilliant blue sky and the crew rowing teams out on the water practicing. I think how Larry would love that.

After a few minutes, I notice this dragonfly fluttering around close to the lake—definitely close enough to see but far enough so that it is out of reach. It has these incredible iridescent pale blue tips to its wings, like no other dragonfly I ever saw before—or maybe it's the play of sunlight on the color. The rest of it is black. I watch it land on a stalk of dried grass, flutter away, come back, and repeat several times. When it leaves for good, I decide that it's time to go, but on my way back I stop and retrieve the feather.

I don't want to leave that there. It belongs with the eagle feather.

I really want/need to cry but the tears just do not come. I return to my room to shower and prepare for the final workshop wrap-up. I turn on my phone and there is a message from last night where friends back home had called just to see how I was doing.

And that brings tears.

The workshop session feels like the ending that it is, and I find that plays on me through the rest of the day. I have lunch with most of the rest of the class and then head off to walk and think. Around five I decide to go get ice cream as a kind of final visit to the terrace (for this trip), and while there I run into someone from class. When she and her husband seem inclined to perhaps include me in their plans for the evening, I surprise myself by confiding that my husband died some weeks ago. In the face of their sympathy, I feel tears coming so I make my excuses, leave them quickly, get my ice cream and find a place to sit alone. After weeks of not being able to cry, suddenly tears are remarkably close.

The music this evening is jazz, usually a genre I enjoy, but tonight I find it unsettling and jarring. I move some distance away, so the music is muted. Checking messages, there is yet another call from friends—this time from Arizona. I decide to call back since I had just missed their call by minutes. When they don't answer and I start leaving a message, once again the tears overflow. In that moment I am relieved not to have reached them.

The tears are accompanied by a feeling of endings and loss that seems as much related to this week coming to an end as it is to grief. For a week now I have been living in another place, away from the rooms and activities that are waiting for my return.

Tomorrow farmer's market, tarot, and home again and then...? In his novel, *Davita's Harp*, Chaim Potok wrote, *There was no feeling more terrible than loneliness; no feeling worse than the sensation of being locked inside your own heart.*

AND JUNE CONTINUES

The week in Madison was exactly what I expected and needed—moments of bitter and moments of sweet; a little pain and a lot of good stuff; new connections made; new lessons learned; and most of all the space and solitude to absorb it all. In short: I am so glad I went.

My return is a new reality—not as difficult coming back into the home we shared as I might have thought but still my only greeting is silence. I get my plant containers resettled into their places after clustering them in one spot so my neighbor could water them and am glad to see that everything survived. Between laundry and phone calls to assure friends I am safely home and doing okay, the day passes.

I awake the following morning and open the shades to look out at the patio and notice for the first time, a lone hollyhock I had forgotten planting in full bloom. I laugh out loud. For years Larry teased me about never wanting me to plant hollyhocks. "They attract bees," he declared with that twinkle that told me he was simply giving me a hard time. It became a running joke between us ... one of so many we shared through the years. Every spring I would plant a hollyhock somewhere in the yard and announce that I had done so. He would react with mock horror. The thing was that no matter how many times I planted them, the hollyhocks *never* bloomed—until now. So, you decide who got the last laugh!

July

The 4th of July and Thanksgiving are my two favorite holidays. In both cases you know what to expect in terms of food and the schedule for the day; you pretty much know what to wear; and there are no gifts involved. Larry was well aware of my preference for these two holidays as well as my love of fireworks. Every summer we looked forward to July with its blooming gardens, picnics, and other gatherings with friends and, of course, fireworks. So, when friends invited me to join them for a neighborhood barbeque on the 4th I was delighted to accept. I picked up another invited couple and headed off. I knew that our hosts had included some neighbors and other friends of theirs that I didn't know but I looked forward to "new blood" in the usual mix of our circle.

And yet just a few hours into the party, I had to find a way to arrange for someone else to drive the couple I had picked up home, slip out of my hosts' house without saying goodbye and barely make it to my car before bursting into sobs.

My tears of grieving have all come at the most unexpected times—none more unexpected than this. Although I admit in hindsight, I became aware of an undercurrent of discomfort early in the evening. I ignored it. All during dinner and the dessert that followed I had laughed with everyone else at oft-told stories from the past, some new adventures from the present and stories of the antics of various grandchildren. Nothing unusual there. In large gatherings, I have a habit of being more of an observer than participant.

Also, I was aware of a certain inner uneasiness when it came to the folks I didn't know—they were all delightful, interesting people and yet I was unsure if they knew that Larry had died so recently. Because I talk freely about him in the company of our close friends, I found myself holding back even though there were stories that would have been appropriate for me to share. If they didn't know I didn't want to put a damper on the festivities and if they did know? Well, same story. On top of that referring to him in the past tense is still difficult.

By the time dessert was being served I realized that I was teetering on the edge. I was aware that my close friends all had a partner plus children plus grandchildren—in short, they had support well beyond friendships. And although we all know families can be dysfunctional—in these cases there is a closeness among the generations that is downright inspirational. Because Larry and I never had children (and obviously no grandchildren) I think what struck me was that absence in my life in a way I had never even considered it before. And the very fact that we don't often get do-overs was emotionally crippling in a way I had not yet faced.

July

In the journal Larry left for me, he raised the fact that we had not had children—sorry in some ways that he was leaving me without that support. But as always reminding me raising a child is a crapshoot at best—his opinion—not mine. Looking back, I remain convinced he would have been a wonderful father. Looking back, I understand I had too much growing up to do myself to shepherd a child.

In the days leading up to this July 4th event I had been feeling pretty proud of the way I was adjusting and finding my way. I am by nature an overachiever. But the words that I found myself repeating over and over as I sat in my car sobbing were, "I don't think I can do this."

So where am I a couple of days past that moment?

Of course, my hosts and those guests who knew me were concerned. They called and I either let the call go to voicemail or, once I felt more in control of my emotions, answered, and downplayed what had happened. Of course, not knowing about the sobbing mess I was in the car, they believed my excuse that I hadn't felt well—something I ate earlier in the day had not agreed with me. They did not see through the deflection and accepted my explanation, offering to bring ginger ale or chicken soup to ease my malady. I could hardly admit that their kindness and caring only made things worse. I have been fooling myself as well as them. It is time to face up to the hard realities of my situation.

I have my writing. I have my friends. I have the comfort of a home and financial security. In short, I have a great deal that I know others may not have. What is missing is that routine—those hours spent at the end of the day catching up and laughing together and yes, sometimes arguing. I talk out loud to Larry every night before I go to sleep, going over the events of the day as I would have if he were here.

The task before me if I am to make it through another week—never mind a full year—is to come to terms with the reality of Larry's death. The two of us were a family unit. Now half of that unit is gone. And I am *not* all right. I have a lot of work to do, and it will take time—a *lot* of time.

MID-JULY

I have just returned from my trip to NYC. Although I had planned to attend a writing conference held there every year, I had moments of doubt that it made sense to attend yet another conference when I had just returned from one in Madison. As a result, I canceled and suddenly the whole trip became more spontaneous up to and including inviting my sister to join me. It has been some time since the two of us spent time together without the buffer of husbands or other family members. I was relieved to find that the connection was immediate, and the visit went well.

The one standout on this trip was a morning spent at the American Folk Art Museum across from Lincoln Center. At the time, the entrance wall to this small museum featured an incredible multi-paneled quilt commemorating those who died on 9/11–on the flights, in the Pentagon, and in the towers. Thousands of small, hand-decorated blocks, each with the name of a victim embroidered on it, made up a tableau forming the skyline of the city with the twin towers set in the palest beige-colored blocks as if they were there once but are no more. I spent some time walking along the length of the tapestry, reading the names, and recalling how I read every single obituary featured in the NY Times in the days and weeks following the attacks. Somehow, I felt a responsibility to know these people at least to the degree that knowing a stranger through a short biographic description is possible. As I studied the quilt, I thought of all these lives, but with my status as one left behind, I was far more focused on the lives their deaths had changed forever.

That night my sister and I attended a big Broadway musical that was the very essence of what many people think when you say "Broadway." It was silly, and kitschy and just plain fun and we walked back to our room humming the Gershwin tunes that made up the music, remembering how as kids we would walk home from seeing a movie like *Singin' in the Rain* reliving the songs and even the dance steps. So, in a single day I had come face-to-face with the sheer ugliness and downright meanness of life on this planet as well as the song-and-dance fantasy world that we sometimes wish were more reality. Oh, how I longed to talk that all through with Larry.

The following morning, I woke early—it was my birthday—a day I do not choose to celebrate as to me it represents the passing of time and a ticking clock. Others do not understand. In fact, they find it all rather ridiculous. But Larry understood that at times like this I needed my aloneness. So, I told my sister I would return in an hour or so and set out for a walk. And as I passed others, I found myself wondering what challenges they might be facing in their lives. One woman I approached to ask directions to a place I thought might be in the neighborhood practically ran from me, her face a mask of anxiety. Clearly a tourist. No New Yorker would be so scared. By contrast a NYC police officer that I approached with the same question pulled out his iPhone and did a map search trying to help.

Later when my sister and I went to Grand Central to get the train to Connecticut to visit a cousin of Larry's for the day, a woman clearly on her way to work approached us and asked if she might help. We were obviously wandering aimlessly around the vast terminal, looking like the lost souls we were. I told her we had over an hour before our train and simply wanted a place to sit. She could have just offered directions but instead she showed us the way to a food court where there was not only a place to sit, but *coffee*!

All of which got me thinking about stereotypes and how in so many ways that is one of the roots of the discord that grows between nations, political adversaries, or people from cities vs. people from more rural settings. If we could just set aside our instinct to label others based on dress, gender, skin color, body language, or geographic location might we not be better equipped to solve problems instead of perpetuating them?

How is this about my journey through widowhood? It goes back to Larry's plea for me to open my mind and heart to the possibility of new relationships and connections. The fact is everything these days is related to this emotional journey I am on because in every situation and experience I find myself searching for clues to the future—who am I without Larry and who will I become?

August

Ramblings . . . in no special order:

Every so often when someone asks how I am doing (and I actually try to briefly describe the pain that defines living without your soulmate), that person will nod sagely and murmur, "I know."

Not "I know it must be so very difficult."

Not "I know you must struggle every hour of every day."

Just "I know."

Well, the fact is that unless they have been there and done that, they *don't* know. They can't even begin to imagine.

Then there are friends. I thought I was prepared for some to surprise and others to disappoint, and at least to some degree, I was. What I wasn't prepared for was *who* would surprise and especially *who* would disappoint, and the hurt I would feel on top of my grief that those friends were not there.

Yet with great guilt and embarrassment I must admit that there are times (rare but still there) when I see the upside of being responsible for and only to myself. I eat when and what I want, go to bed and get up when I want, open the windows and doors when I want, arrange the house the way I want.

But that's small comfort for the loss of those moments when Larry and I laughed together and cried together and held each other. When I was in the airport waiting to board my flight home, an elderly couple came walking by. He pushed her wheelchair and when they had found a place to wait, he took her hand. In that moment, I realized that closeness, that simple gesture that says "I am right here" is one of the small seemingly insignificant gestures I miss the most.

Looking over the last several entries, I realize how much I have traveled this first summer, and now have to wonder if I am running away from the real work of grieving. Or am I simply exploring possibilities for what life might look like going forward? I had once planned to write a book I called *365 Days in NYC*, and research it by going to NYC and living for a year. Larry loved the idea and encouraged me to pursue it once he was gone. Unfortunately, my agent did not agree. She correctly pointed out I had no credentials for writing such a book. The fact that has never stopped me before has me questioning why I allowed her "expert opinion" to stop me now.

AUGUST–STARTING TO SEE SIGNS OF AUTUMN

There have already been a number of "firsts" but perhaps tonight was the most startling first of all when I realized that on this ordinary night I cooked. This is the first conventional meal that I have prepared since Larry died. Granted, it was just some scrambled eggs, veggies, and cheese, but it is the first time I have made

August

anything resembling a traditional supper for myself. Either I eat out or I fix myself a bowl of cereal or cut some cheese and fruit, but I have not cooked anything for three months now. My appetite has been weak although I have lost zero weight—a clear indication that in "grazing" and grabbing whatever strikes me in the moment I am not doing myself any favors. Larry would definitely be upset with the way I've been eating—he wouldn't say anything but oh, the looks he could give me! The truth is I like to cook—for others. But maybe I need to cook for me or lose the ability to make good food. The problem is for me food has always been fuel—something I grab when my reserves of energy are running low, and by definition foods that are at hand are rarely healthy.

In another first I went to the State Fair—a tradition we never missed even last summer when Larry was really struggling. This time I went with his sister and our niece, and we had a good time, but it was so hugely different. There was so much that Larry and I liked to do that didn't happen this year, mostly because as always, I was trying to do whatever his sister and our niece wanted. I did have our traditional chocolate "nog," a sample of maple cotton candy, and a glass of cherry vanilla milk. And I did ride the sky glider, so not all was lost. And perhaps the bonus was that as the day ended, I felt closer to my sister-in-law and niece.

Part of my new normal is assuming responsibility for all the financial tasks Larry managed. Tomorrow, I transfer the first of the multiple IRAs. I am not at all sure of the best way to handle this, but tonight I will explore options as I did with the CDs and then decide. Hopefully, Larry will be there with me, so I don't make some huge mistake. Yes, there are friends I could ask who would be happy to offer advice, but one thing Larry and I shared was the need for privacy when it came to our finances. Clearly our approach to such matters differed. My inclination is to consolidate my investments while he spent hours seeking out the most attractive interest rates, meaning our money was scattered among numerous banks around the city. I understand the potential risks of placing all these (nest)eggs in one basket but having everything where our investment advisor can keep watch seems worth that risk.

Assuming I survive the trauma that is the constant fear I will make some huge monetary mistake, perhaps I'll go to the grocery store and instead of perusing the salad bar and deli selections, I'll buy some "real" food and come home and make a proper dinner—just like I used to do.

Postscript: A proper dinner never happened. What's that saying about good intentions?

MORE AUGUST
Already three months feels like thirty years. I promised myself that I would not stalk anniversaries (quarter of a year; half a year; etc.) but that's impossible to avoid when well-meaning friends remind me. Of course, it's all in the best sense of caring and concern, but still, it brings on some heavy-duty loneliness. I have to wonder how people not as blessed as I am to be surrounded by a network of friends and the security that comes with having worked and saved for times like these get through at all.

There's a real danger of falling into the trap of thinking I am unique in this—of failing to see and understand there are so many others who are either experiencing what I am or who have already weathered years of this overwhelming loneliness and doubt. In some cases, these are not random strangers to me—there are friends who have also traveled these painful first months—who indeed know all too well at least a bit of what I have faced already and what lies ahead.

It is so important I do not ignore or forget their pain and grief. Just because they are farther down the road does not lessen the loss.

As always, I find solace in my work, not to mention some escape. Rearranging my surroundings is another distraction. Yesterday I spent four hours switching the living room furniture with the furniture in the family room. As I stood back admiring my handiwork, I recalled how Larry used to tease me that he would never dare come home in the dark because he never knew if the sofa would be where the kitchen table used to be or vice versa.

And once again I understand that the hardest part of this journey will always be not having him here—to talk to about serious or silly things, about things like perceived slights or wounds that would drive him nuts, about things that made him smile, about things that I really do not want to talk to anyone else about—no matter how dear a friend they might be.

I guess in some ways I put that backwards because as I have noted before, I do talk to him all the time. But, of course, what I hear is the sound of my own voice. Larry was always a quiet man, a man of few words, but how I long to just hear his laugh, see him nod his head, see his frown of disapproval—I would take anything!

Okay, beginning to whine and wallow.

And then I remember in the months before he died, Larry made tape recordings of him looking at one of the albums from trips we had taken and talking about the photos and journal I always kept. He did this while I was away, usually at my studio. A friend whose husband had died suddenly several years earlier had given him the idea. She told him one thing she missed most was the sound of her husband's voice. Another friend gave Larry a voice-activated recorder, and I have this treasure trove of recordings, often interrupted by him taking a phone call and sometimes just him talking to me about what my life might be going forward. I have these

The "W" Word

wonderful "conversations"—one-sided to be sure—but his voice and laughter are right there for me to listen to any time I wish.

September

I don't like roller coasters and other such thrill rides, but clearly this is going to be a journey of hurtling ups and downs. There are entire weeks that go by when I feel as if I'm adjusting pretty well.

And then...

This week I went to see my doctor because of an unusual shot of pain I felt in my leg. Never one to get overly upset about a health issue, I now find that almost any symptom I cannot explain away immediately raises concerns. I know it has to do with living alone—the fear of something happening, not having anyone else in the house and not being able to call for help. And yet, I am not ready to surrender to wearing the *I've-fallen-and-can't-get-up* alarm system.

As usual the nurse took my blood pressure upon arrival (right after weighing me). Why do they persist in that order of things especially for women? Most of us hate stepping on a scale under any circumstances. Why on earth would anyone think BP might be normal after such stress?

But, once again, I digress.

The doctor examined me and eased my mind about the leg issue. It was likely a pinched nerve. She made a referral for me to have an assessment by a physical therapist. Once I had a plan of action, I immediately felt more in control. But then when I got home, I had a voicemail from my doctor saying she had tried to catch me before I left because after reviewing my BP, she would have liked to have taken it again. Of course, this was late on a Friday before the Labor Day weekend. Long story short: I went to a walk-in clinic and had it repeated. It was still high, so I dragged out the home BP cuff to check it myself over the holiday weekend. Readings were all over the map, making me suspect the cuff was not working properly.

My medical community has an online communications system where I can see test results, contact my doctor, take online evaluations, and get prevention information. So, I took what they called a stress measurement—this is not the physical measure where you walk on a treadmill but rather a checklist where you mark the things going on in your life that could cause stress.

I was off the charts.

And that surprised me because I thought that I was doing rather well for what I am going through and the fact that it hasn't been that long. Of course, that set me up for even more stress as I obsessed about a possible stroke or heart attack and being alone and not being able to get help in time and . . . and . . . and. . . .

On Sunday morning I woke at 5:30 with something akin to a panic attack; got up and took my BP med and baby aspirin; tried to sit quietly and meditate; then went out to collect the newspaper from end of the driveway.

September

I almost didn't make it back inside because of weakness and dizziness. Finally, I decided to face this the way I have faced pretty much everything scary in my life—I took action—on my own. Not the smartest choice when it comes to health issues, but it's who I am.

I found an open local care clinic and had them do a reading which was the highest yet. I took my home BP cuff along and the numbers were comparable, but did that mean I could trust the home reading? Once home I called the doctor but of course, it's a holiday weekend so talked instead to the nurse on call. She had me do a reading with my cuff—much better.

What is going on here?

The nurse's advice was to calm down, relax, take a walk, or go be with friends, maybe see a movie, check BP at home every three to four hours, watch for symptoms such as headache, dizziness, or weakness on one side and call doctor on Tuesday after the holiday. Still unsettled, I called a friend who is a pharmacist who told me the blood pressure medication I've been on forever is really the mildest form of treatment so presumably my doctor will up the dosage or order something stronger. In the meantime, he assured me that I am not likely to stroke out or die—the former being the more dreaded in my book, having witnessed the arduous battle Larry faced following his stroke.

I saw the doctor the following week and got the recommended change in medication that sent my blood pressure back to normal and allowed me to keep moving forward. So physically, all is well. Mentally and emotionally? Not so much.

MID-SEPTEMBER

Our Florida friend came for a visit over the weekend. From his arrival last Friday until he left yesterday morning, we were pretty much on the go and surrounded by others who wanted to see him and catch up. We spent a wonderful—albeit cold and rainy—day in Madison. We went with another couple and visited the farmer's market, some campus hangouts from their days at the university and the place where last summer I left some of Larry's ashes along the lake path. We pretty much ate our way through Sunday—a wonderful brunch with friends and then supper with other friends—but the stories, memories and laughter were the richest part of the menu.

It is so comforting for me that when friends speak of Larry it's always with such genuine delight at having known this marvelous man. They miss him as I do—his male friends especially long for the opportunity to rehash a football game or other sporting event with him or dissect the latest political or business fiasco. But their shared memories bring only smiles and a kind of peace. And I fully appreciate for perhaps the first time that when someone dies, it is not just the immediate family who deserves the understanding that grief is difficult. Friends—and in some cases, even co-workers or business associates—will also have their moments.

On Monday I cooked for the football party our friend and I were hosting that night while he tackled some outside painting that Larry had asked him to do whenever he got here for a visit. Then he helped me set everything up. I realized how much I missed having another person here to bounce things off—would it be best to set the food here or there? Would there be enough food? All the stuff I would have fretted over with Larry. And even though our team suffered a last second loss, the evening was wonderful despite it—a house filled with friends and laughter and moans and groans and good food as it always was when Larry was here.

And somehow, I know that he was.

October

Five months in and it occurs to me that this journey—like many passages in life—is all about making choices. Each choice becomes its own destination—its own little postcard moment. Some of the choices are routine—for example, when to eat, what to eat, where to eat.

When Larry was alive, every evening around six we sat at the dining room table. It was more spacious and had a better view than our small kitchen table. The meal was well-rounded: usually fish or chicken, rice or potato, veggie, salad. If there was going to be dessert it came later as we watched TV. Up until about two years ago Larry might have been the one preparing the meal. When he retired at age 50 because his health was beginning to fail even then, I went to work in the corporate world mostly for the health insurance we needed to get to Medicare age. That was when he began making supper three nights a week.

This evening meal was the only meal of the day we shared. As we ate, we would talk about all the things that had happened that day—in the world, in the workplace, in the neighborhood, among friends, and most of all with us. Or we would discuss short or long-term plans for the future. Over four decades of marriage, we never once lacked for conversation.

Now that I am alone, I find I need to make different choices. These days the dining room table is often covered with some project I'm working on—bills and bank statements and such that need attention; my latest writing project; lists I make to be sure I take care of everything now that he's not here to remind me or handle it himself. So, meals—such as they are—are more often consumed while watching TV or catching up on email. Blessedly I go out with friends at least once a week for a "real" meal.

Although I thought when this all began that eventually I would settle into some kind of routine for eating normal meals again, I can see that this is unlikely. The choice has been made—not the best choice perhaps but one that for now works for me. As I mentioned before for me food has always been more a jolt of energy than something to be savored. I have little interest in dissecting the contents—which spices have given it that flavor and so forth. I am as happy with a bowl of cereal as I am with fine dining—maybe more so. Not a good thing—just a true thing.

OCTOBER CONTINUES

As I had expected, once the hustle and bustle of handling details—financial, home maintenance, plans for immediate events—lessened, the reality that I am the one now making decisions and handling chores I gave little thought to in the past settles over me like a dense fog. A contributing factor to my slide into a darker place is that from the time I was eight or nine I found the season of October-November depressing and sad so that doesn't exactly bode well for slogging through these days in a year that is anything but normal.

Yes, his spirit is with me but that is not at all the same. I can't curl into the side of his spirit the way I used to; I can't discuss frustrations with all the details that come with handling the house maintenance—workers not calling back or not showing up; I can't go through the financial stuff with him to be sure I am doing it right. Yes, there are others in my life I could turn to but it's not even close to the same. They have their way and it's not Larry's way—or for that matter, mine.

So tough times right now. I know this too shall pass but that's small comfort. The truth is that I feel like I am simply moving through the hours—continuing to accept the dwindling invitations that come my way and tell myself how blessed I am to have people who care. I know that things could be ever so much worse for me. Larry used that argument whenever I started to whine and feel sorry for myself. I would fire back that we were not talking about "other people" and their problems. We were talking about me and what was going on in my head. Guilting me out of it never worked—and it doesn't work now although I'll admit that I am deeply ashamed of myself for not focusing on what *is* rather than what isn't.

No real conclusion to this, other than the reality that grief is work—hard exhausting work.

MORE OCTOBER

Just back from Chicago—part business and part memory lane. Chicago is where Larry and I fell in love, and it has always been incredibly special to me for several reasons. So, when I had the chance to go into the city for business I decided to stay overnight.

While there I visited locations that were all landmarks of the times we shared. Most of the places are no longer physically there—like where I worked and lived—but the neighborhoods remain and so do the memories. Wonderful, detailed memories of laughter and tears and long walks and serious talks and just being young and falling in love.

I am realizing with the passing of each day how especially important it is to look back and appreciate all we shared. Not in a maudlin, sorrowful way. Rather in a way that makes me smile at the memories and even from time to time brings on the tears. They are tears of sadness, of course. But they are also tears of appreciation for the time we had, and the fact that for the most part, we did not waste it. I understand now that each day was a treasure. Sometimes we missed seeing the treasure in the moment, but the number of days we spent fully aware of just how fortunate we were to have found each other far outdistances those days when we forgot.

How do I explain a love story so fulfilling that it has indeed continued beyond the grave? I had him in body for over four decades, but I am beginning to understand that I will have him in spirit for eternity.

November

Finally. Meaning I can distract myself from the doldrums that come with autumn by starting to prepare for winter in Florida. I had promised Larry that I would go back for at least one more season. My feelings about Florida are mixed, as selfish as that may sound to those facing winter winds, ice and snow!

We started wintering in Florida eight years ago, and it did not take long that first season for me to face two hard realities: 1) Larry's health was deteriorating and the best we could hope for was to cling to the status quo for as long as possible. So short of a medical miracle, there would be no chance for improvement. 2) Going to Florida meant we were mostly done traveling—except for brief weekend getaways closer to home. So, I am not at all certain how I will feel about being there now. Of course, I understand that I am free to come and go as I please, and I am grateful our wonderful network of friends and family continues down there.

But it's going to be yet another new adjustment, and I am so very weary of facing new challenges that test my coping skills.

On a more positive front, I stumbled across a wonderful memoir the other day. *Grieving: A Love Story* is Ruth Coughlin's account of her journey through widowhood. A couple of quotes from the fly leaf illustrate how spot on her observations are:

No one can tell you about grief, about its limitless boundaries, its unfathomable depths.... No one can tell you about the crater that is created ... the one that nothing can fill.

There's no right or wrong to widowhood; nobody's written the rules.... You make them up as you go along.

I hear you, lady—loud and clear!

MID-NOVEMBER

My entry back into Florida has been a bit chaotic. First, arriving on a Sunday, I could not get into the apartment and had to call a locksmith since my landlords are in Maryland. Then the car that was scheduled to arrive Tuesday at the latest did not arrive until Thursday and was unloaded covered with mud in the turn lane of a busy thoroughfare. It wasn't so much the extra days in transit that bothered me but rather the fact that neither the driver nor the company responded to my calls or let me know there had been a delay. They had my car loaded with my stuff and I could not reach them. I couldn't help thinking this is something Larry would have handled brilliantly while I was a basket case.

But by the end of the week everything was in place and this piece of the journey began in earnest on November 9th ... six months ... half a year ... seems like yesterday ... seems like a lifetime ... seems impossible.

The issues here are no different than they were back home. The days are filled with activity and work, and just like in Wisconsin, it

November

is the evenings that are hardest, even those evenings when I spend a couple of hours enjoying dinner or a play with friends. I still come back to an empty place. I try to take a long walk every day and get to the beach to walk at least several times a week.

On my walk yesterday, I was thinking about Larry's aversion to the use of the term "lost" to refer to a death. It occurred to me that he understood that it is not the person who died who is "lost" but rather those left behind. I am the one who is lost, wandering around trying to determine who I am now that half of me is missing. And yes, I know I've said that before—several times. The point is it's a thought that recurs when I least expect it—when I have told myself I am doing better.

As I wrestle with what this me-without-Larry will look like and sound like and act like, I realize that I have this unique opportunity. For years now I have been in what a friend whose husband also died following a long illness calls "caregiving mode." She pointed out it didn't just extend to Larry. It was the way I dealt with everyone—acquiescing to their wishes, their needs, their preferences. In truth there rarely seemed to be anything I felt worth standing my ground for. Every day was a struggle to try and make life as good as possible for Larry, to keep family and friends engaged and, in the loop, and to try and maintain my sanity in the process.

But now I have this unique opportunity to turn my attention to me, to care for my needs, my preferences, my new self. To be sure, this is foreign territory for even as a kid, my focus was on pleasing others. Shifting the focus to *me* sounds incredibly self-centered. Yet I cannot deny that if there is anything positive in all of this, it is the sense of freedom I feel. There's the sensation that after years of caring for my parents and helping care for my sister and Larry's mother, followed by the years of his own failing health, I am relieved of responsibility to others.

Please do *not* misread this—Larry was nowhere close to a controlling man—definitely *not* a my-way-or-the-highway kind of guy. He was always focused on others but what I have realized is that the logistics of being a couple is based on consideration of the partner's needs and wishes. Now that I am alone, the rule no longer applies. And that in its way is a miniscule positive in a sea of negatives that go with missing the one person you built your life around and with. Still, it is a positive and I can maybe find a way to nurture that . . . and myself.

December

One of the quirks about this journey is the use of pronouns. When did "we" become just "I" and "our" become just "my"? I'm not sure others pay much attention, but I am so very aware that when I say something like "Come on over to ____ house after the game…" I am hesitating before choosing the pronoun. In my heart it is *our* house and always will be. Even though here in Florida, it is a rented condo, it is the place where we shared so many significant and silly times. It, like the condo we own in Milwaukee, is the repository of memories. Perhaps one day I will live somewhere that I did not share with Larry, but will the address really matter? If the structure is furnished with "our" things, won't it still be ours?

Then there is "we" vs. "I." This one kind of works because it seems natural to use past tense with we as in "We always loved to…" or "One time we were…" If someone extends an invite it's also pretty natural to simply say "I'd love to…" Clearly, I'm not yet so lost that I have fantasies that "we" could accept. So, it is the possessive that gives me pause. But underlying this struggle in semantics is a deeper more painful coming to terms with the fact that these days only the past is "our" and "we". The present and the future are both single . . . I . . . me . . . my.

The so-called "pronoun" trend that has developed over the last several years has always confused and frustrated me. I get that it has to do with gender identity, but for me it divides more than connects. When pushed, I will declare my "pronouns" to always be we—us—ours. Inclusive. Connected. A whole rather than a piece.

MID-DECEMBER

My heart is breaking for the families of those killed in yet another school shooting and horrific massacre—and not just the children but also the adult victims who had families of their own who are also in such pain. I know there has been a lot of talk about gun control measures, and I applaud that. It is past time. My family had guns and I have shot at targets myself, so I am not anti-gun or hunting or home protection. That said, do we really need a gun to shoot a gazillion bullets a minute, or bullets that are capable of penetrating a metal file cabinet stuffed with files to hit their victim?

And beyond that I agree with those who say that gun control is only the first step of many. For example, we decimated our mental health system for budget reasons years ago, and we continue to pay a heavy price for that. It's not just in these terrible and shocking events, but also in the everyday lives of our friends and neighbors who may be suffering and in pain mentally and emotionally. Our schools struggle to offer programs such as music, art, drama and even sports that can truly reach a child in pain. And now will more programs be cut to cover the costs of security?

Events like this are yet another reminder that I am far from alone in suffering and grieving, that in many ways I had the blessing of time to say my goodbye when others do not. These parents sent their child off to school one morning, never for one moment imagining they would die there. Thinking about this humbles me and gives me a greater appreciation for how fortunate Larry and I were. In that same vein, I continue to try and look for the positives as I make this journey. Friends and family may not always come through in the ways I would like, but they are there. And I find comfort in the memories of decades of love, and the "gifts" Larry left me of a journal and voice recordings. Most of all there is my own inner strength gained from my upbringing and my faith that keep me in balance. Over these last months, I have spoken to and read about many dealing with emotional pain, and I am struck by their courage and determination to see that through to a better day.

I am writing this in the "season of giving," although any time of year is the right time for looking for ways to reach out to others, not just by donating a can of food or writing a check in December but face to face. Year-round. We are surrounded by others who are suffering, struggling or in pain. One thing I have learned beyond doubt in these last months is that the times I reach out to others and focus on their need rather than my own, those are the times when, for just a moment, I forget my own sadness and pain.

CHRISTMAS DAY

From last night's Eve service, a quote by theologian Howard Thurman:

> When the song of the angels is stilled
> When the star in the sky is gone
> When the kings and princes are home

The "W" Word

> When the shepherds are back with their flock
> The work of Christmas begins:
> to find the lost
> to heal the broken
> to feed the hungry
> to release the prisoner
> to rebuild the nations
> to bring peace among people
> to make music in the heart.

My first holiday season without Larry has been an eye-opening experience filled with unexpected surprises and "gifts" in the form of calls and cards from so many, a visit from two people I have had contact with for years but am just beginning to deeply appreciate, family, friends, tears, and laughter. It has indeed been a joyous season, a time for reflection on the wonderful life I have been given. And always *always* the realization that Larry continues to be with me in spirit if not in body, and for that I am so very thankful.

January

And so, I have made it through the holidays. I feel the comfort of Larry's emotional presence with me in almost everything I do and over the last week or so have only really had one emotional skid.

That's progress.

One thing I am learning is that my new identity gives me some interesting privileges. One example: friends here annually host a New Year's Eve party. In the past it would be unthinkable not to attend, and yet, when I told the hostess I just wasn't ready, she understood and made no attempt to dissuade me. That kind of acceptance from others that things are not the same for me and I need time reminds me how fortunate I am to have others who are ready to accept my decisions even in times when they may think a party with friends is exactly what I need.

So, as I sat here last night quietly bringing in the New Year it occurred to me that true to my nature, I have unknowingly created a kind of checklist of things I need to take care of before I can focus on my own future. Of course, no one has inferred that I need to do these things. They are strictly self-inflicted. But they are part of the path I feel I must follow to lead me to my new future.

Little stuff, perhaps even stupid stuff like organizing not only my studio and condo back in Wisconsin but also this place that I rent here in Florida. This morning was spent reorganizing the space where the beach toys/chairs, etc. are stored to make them more accessible to those who stay here. I never use those things but perhaps the next renters will. There's also the must-do stuff like preparing the tax information for the accountant and praying I get it right! And always the good-for-me-in-spite-of-myself stuff like joining an exercise program that pushes me to show up and do the work because I paid a fair amount of money for it.

Nothing huge. Just normal life, and I do get it that the list will likely change and continue to grow and will never truly be done. The good news is that on this first day of a new year, I do feel as if I am moving forward. Not that I don't have my furious-at-the-unfairness-of-it-all times. If Larry taught me anything it was that this is the moment, not the hour or day—but the *moment* we get, so use it well or lose it forever.

And in this moment, it is a gloriously sunny warm day, and I will not lose it. I am in Florida when I could be in the near-zero chill of Wisconsin.

Life is good.

I'm going to the beach.

JANUARY–A WEEK LATER

Having created this checklist in my head of things I feel compelled to do, I need to actually attend to that list. These are not things anyone else *expects* me to do. They are completely self-imposed.

January

Still, I find the ability to check them off one by one incredibly therapeutic—even if there is an element of procrastination embedded in some of the items on the list—like the exercise pledge.

In addition to the checklist, there have been other recent moments of healing. My brother and sister-in-law came to visit, and for the three nights they were here we probably grew closer than we've been in years. Each night we sat out on the balcony and talked until past midnight, catching up on the years we had not shared. A week later I went with a group of friends to Sanibel Island off the Gulf Coast of Florida for a long weekend of shelling. The tides were supposed to be especially low during this time and that usually bodes well for finding treasures on the beach. We were up and out before daylight most mornings—flashlights in hand. But the truly special parts of that was shutting off the lights and just standing on the beach looking up at the sky—black with billions of stars. It was so inspiring, so indicative of our insignificance in the great universe.

While others engaged in bridge or mahjong games, I spent hours walking the beaches where Larry and I planned out huge chunks of our life together. So many memories created on those walks. Finally last weekend I traveled to visit friends south of here who had for the last several years always come to us because Larry could not handle the travel. It was strange driving some distance by myself, and it's still hard being a "single" when we are out to eat, but overall, it was a good visit with wonderful friends who have played significant roles in my life.

February

Moving forward—some might say at warp speed.

It all started a few weeks ago when I went to look at a condo here in Sarasota in a wonderful old 1920's building that I have admired since Larry and I started coming down here. I had been playing around online looking at various condo offerings because I thought my sister was looking for a place and this one came up. It was totally wrong for her, but I couldn't get it off my mind. I had no intention of ever buying a second home anywhere. Larry and I always thought that what I would do once he died was travel abroad since we had been unable to do that as much as we'd once hoped. But I've discovered over the last several months that travel is nice but it's not at all that key to my current happiness.

After looking at the photos of this condo every night, I finally told myself that I should go see it. I rationalized that the online pictures always make a place look better than it really is and that by going to see it I would be able to get it off my mind.

So wrong!

What happened next was an utterly stunning and spiritual experience that proved to be the beginning of an adventure I would never have guessed would be part of this journey.

Even before crossing the threshold of the place, I had already discovered one humongous downside: no elevator. But once inside the front door with the charming Old-World transom above, I found myself bathed in sunlight in a place with the honey-colored wood floors, lofty ceilings and period details that speak to my love of history. More to the point, for the first time since Larry died, I felt such a sense of peace and calm and happiness. Genuine happiness was a feeling I almost couldn't recognize because I had been sad and faking it for months, but whatever this was, I felt *good*!

I wandered through the rooms, delighting in the discovery of charming nooks and mentally replacing the furnishings with my own. I actually found myself giggling with delight. Long story a little shorter I began the process of making an offer, against the advice of our real estate attorney friend, who warned me living in a place listed on the National Register of Historic Buildings could come with all sorts of hidden costs and assessments. As it turned out, a moot point since, after a bit of back and forth, I lost the opportunity to live there to another buyer.

Still, I couldn't stop thinking about that moment when everything felt so right. On a walk one evening, I happened by a house I recalled admiring with Larry. Then it had been for sale and was open the day we passed by. He insisted I go in and have a look around—alone. He would wait for me. After I took the tour and we continued our walk, he told me he could see me one day finding a place of my own. I had forgotten all about that day, but now felt so strongly that this was something I was supposed to do that I visited an open house in the complex where we have always rented. While this place did not come close to the wonderful character and history of that lovely old vintage building, it had several features the other place did not, like an elevator and a large private balcony. In my quest to recapture that initial feeling I had experienced in the vintage apartment, I realized that for me space of my own has always been a key to my inner peace and happiness. I love my landlord and feel so at home in her condo. Through the years she has given me lots of freedom to make it as much mine as it is hers. She even refers to it as "our" place. But realizing I could indeed have a place that would be mine, not ours, I made an offer.

A day later, the sellers countered, and, after talking to my financial planner and tax accountant to make sure I wasn't completely crazy, I countered back with my absolute bottom-line offer. The sellers turned that down.

Both deals had failed, and I was bewildered. In my mind I had already rearranged the furniture that came with the place and been to the local consignment store to scout out one or two extra pieces I felt would put my stamp on things. I knew the search was over at least for this season because in a few weeks I would return to Wisconsin. I had a good cry as I took a long walk on the beach. Later I talked to myself about the importance of letting this go and focusing on the realities of what I needed to get done over the next few weeks. The list was daunting—taxes, a book deadline, revisions on another book, packing for the trip North, getting the car shipped. The following morning, I went to breakfast with friends, thankful that I had not confided my house hunt to others. At least I did not need to field their questions about what had gone wrong or if I would continue to look or was I sure this was a good idea. That certainty that this was what I needed to do seemed an illusion, but I reminded myself that many people out there would love to have my "problems."

A few days later—Valentine's Day—the broker called to say the sellers had reconsidered and would like to accept my final offer. I asked for time to think it over, knowing already that I would agree. This felt as if Larry was sending me a special gift. That feeling of breathing out and filling up with joy was back. My friends and family were in shock. "You did what?" "It hasn't been a year, maybe...." Their shocked facial expressions mirrored the doubt I heard in their gentle attempts urging me to give this more thought. But I knew that I had made the right decision and had just taken a huge step toward defining the life I would live now that Larry is gone.

LATE FEBRUARY–LARRY'S BIRTHDAY

Today about two dozen friends and I held a second memorial celebration of Larry's life—it was fitting that it came on his actual birthday. He had asked me to be sure to do something here in Florida for those friends who could not come to Wisconsin last May and to once again make sure it was a celebration. What a wonderful event it turned out to be!

The Ringling Bridge runs from mainland Sarasota over to the barrier islands. Every year Larry made several trips biking up and over that bridge and back again. Toward the end of the season our last year, he came back one day and said, "I made it to the top of the bridge today." I knew that was the only time that season he had managed that and that it was also the final time. Sure enough that was the day he stopped riding his bike.

So, taking that trip on foot with friends who had loved him as I did seemed a fitting memorial. Together we made the long gradual climb to the top of the bridge where we stood for a moment in silence and then dropped orchid and rose petals into the aqua waters of Sarasota Bay far below. Because of the strong wind the petals flew through the air scattering out onto the water as they landed. One person noted the petals looked like a swarm of butterflies, and it was true. It was so beautiful, and I was not the only one with tears in my eyes as we walked back.

Afterwards we had lunch at Larry's favorite pizza place. I had given the chef there his recipe for the salmon patties he used to make as one of his standard suppers when he cooked for us. To my delight, the chef took the recipe and produced appetizer sized patties for us to enjoy. I had also ordered Larry's favorite frozen custard along with hot fudge and caramel sauce sent from Wisconsin for dessert. It was a day filled with stories and laughter—a bittersweet day to be sure—but as always with Larry the emphasis was on the sweet.

March

The month is almost gone, and it has been some time since I wrote and much has happened. I kept my promise to return to Florida for the winter—and how different that all turned out from what I thought it would be when I arrived last November. If nothing else, I realized that sorting out my life while walking on a sunny beach is certainly preferable to plowing through slush and snow under gray skies.

By arriving in Florida before my other snowbird friends, I had time to connect with the new friends Larry and I have found in Florida over the last several years. Another widow who I have admired greatly but known only casually asked to have dinner with me. I was curious to talk to her about her experiences now that she's several years out from the death of her husband. He, like Larry, suffered for several years and my friend was cast in the role of caregiver as was I. Over fish tacos at our favorite restaurant, I learned that much of what I have experienced was similar to what she had gone through in her early days. Following that dinner, we went to a couple of movies together and in general connected on a level we had not known before. I knew that Larry would be so pleased because he admired and respected this woman so very much, and because in reaching out to her I had done something that used to be completely out of character for me.

I was changing.

Then there were "the guys." As everyone settled into our snowbird life, Larry's male friends began including me in their conversation whenever the group gathered to watch sports. Their respect for my interest in sports touched me greatly, and the escape from what I will call the kitchen chatter about food and grandkids and such was frankly a relief. When Larry was alive, I often retreated to the circle of men, curling up next to Larry on a sofa as I listened to talk of players and recruits and chances for championships. But with Larry no longer there, I had retreated to what I believed must be my place now that I was alone. I was so delighted when I realized those engaged in the sport of the day did not see it that way at all.

But of course, the biggest surprise of all came when I went to look at that vintage condo—mostly out of curiosity and an interest in the building's historic roots. From that experience and the days that followed I learned what I really needed was that room of my own as Virginia Woolf once called it. I most assuredly understand most people in my position cannot salve their grief by buying real estate. But that is not the point. What happened here was that something pushed me in a new direction. I turned a corner and saw before me the possibility that once I turn dozens and perhaps thousands of corners, I will find my way.

March

Now that I am back in Wisconsin, I will admit that there has been a sense of letdown. The excitement and angst of my time in Florida is over for the time being. Did my Florida adventure make a difference? In that moment, it did. Going forward, only time will tell.

April

Excellence—excelling at some task—was something I was taught throughout my life. It is a trait ingrained in me, a trait I know some would think of as competitive. But I am driven to get things right and this "W" thing is no exception.

Since returning from Florida, I have struggled more and more. I could say it's the weather over the last several weeks in Wisconsin. It has been unceasingly gray, gloomy, and cold with wet snow that turns into piles of slush blocking curbside drains. There are also the bone-chilling dampness and sharp winds off Lake Michigan. Even if it's too warm to snow, there has been so much rain that a person might seriously consider building an ark. And I suppose there is an element of the weather that contributes to the downward slide I have made emotionally and spiritually these last weeks. The fact that I have been fighting bronchitis for several days now and that I have a deadline for my next book looming have been major contributors to my feelings of depression. All valid assumptions.

I suddenly understand at the heart of all my angst lies a single truth: I am so very tired of starting over, of having to adapt my life to circumstances not of my own making, of finding a way to move forward. I have choices I can make, roads I can take or not, self-pity that I can either wallow in or reject. And as has been said, failure to act is in and of itself an action. There have been any number of times in my life when starting over was my only choice. Examples include a time in my college days when I had mapped out a future with a career working in government and marriage to my college sweetheart. In my mind, these were a given, but neither happened. Later years brought the assumption Larry and I would have a family. That, too, was not meant to be. Most recently, of course, the happy future Larry and I had spent so much time imagining disintegrated into where I am today.

My therapist has told me several times that Albert Einstein's definition of insanity is doing the same thing the same way time and again and expecting a different result. I do that a lot—always going back to the same perceived slights and issues I wish had turned out differently. It is way past time to let go of that kind of pettiness. Larry always counseled that. It made him so incredibly sad that I would be better for a time but would eventually circle back around to whining about the same old stuff.

In the play *A Raisin in the Sun,* there is dialogue about how life is not a circle but an unending line. It is a line we cannot see the finish of and one we can only move along addressing the situation we find ourselves in at this singular moment. We can, of course, plan for the future, but always with the full understanding that those plans may change—or be changed.

I was married to a man who knowing all this with a certainty that most of us never have, *chose* to live his life with grace and humor, *chose* to place the focus of his days on me and on others; *chose* to have no regrets when the end came because he knew that he had done everything he could for as long as he could. He had never given up but rather adapted to the changing circumstances that the reality of his limits dictated.

Surely in honoring his memory and a life so well lived, I, too, must learn to let go and move forward with purpose so that whenever my end may come, I will be able to look back without regret. Larry's mantra was *It is what it is.* After he died, I heard an interview with University of Tennessee basketball coach, Pat Summitt, who had recently been diagnosed with Alzheimer's. She added a line, saying, "It is what it is, and it will be what I make of it."

May

Yesterday was a tough day, and I still have the anniversary looming. I am aware the entries in this written journey are getting shorter and less frequent. I wonder if that in itself is a sign of healing.

Physically I continue to feel lousy, fighting a variety of symptoms that leave me exhausted and out of sorts. I had just received the galley proof for my next book and needed to read through it before sending it off to the editor. The weather was beautiful and eighty degrees, but I was chilled all day.

I missed the excitement I had experienced In Florida in finding and buying the condo, in moving in and making the furnishings it came with mine, of rising in the morning and sitting on my balcony with coffee, delighting in the fact that I had done this—on my own. Now back in Wisconsin, once again, I was not only missing the sunshine and excitement of new adventures, but I was also feeling physically unsettled, as if some unseen shoe was about to drop. And again, as I focused on the possibility of some health disaster, I was struck by the absence of anyone else in the house to commiserate or act as a safety net should things take a turn for the worse. I have many people that I could call starting with neighbors and moving on to family and friends. But the very idea I would *need* to call someone is incredibly uncomfortable for me. Because I am overall a healthy person this realization that there probably will come a day when I have no choice but to rely on others is devastating. And yet I can't expect others to read my mind. When I had Larry and didn't need anyone else, I saw that as a good thing since over my lifetime so many I have trusted have let me down. But I don't have him anymore. This is the hardcore reality of widowhood that must be faced, not once, but repeatedly.

Another thought I had today concerned choices made or rejected: I was driving past a haircut place that had posted a sign for a sale on haircuts, and I remembered that this was where Larry had gone for his last haircut about this time last year. But that was not what came immediately to mind. What I remembered was how he charmed the woman cutting his hair, and how when she said she was putting the settings for the clippers into their computer system so they would know next time he came in, he smiled and agreed—knowing there would be no next time but choosing not to burden her with that news. It is the memory of a moment like this that makes me determined to re-examine myself. How would I have responded in that same situation?

So, it is all about choices. Larry knew and practiced that. I am trying, with limited success, to follow his example.

MAY–A DIFFERENT ANNIVERSARY

Hard to miss the fact that today marks one year since Larry's death. Friends have been overwhelmingly concerned as the day approached. Today there have been calls and cards and wonderful vibes of their love and support.

Last night I found myself reliving those final hours, counting my blessings that I was with him, and that it was just the two of us at home as he had always wanted. I also found myself looking back over this last year and realizing how I have found my way. Sometimes that came with sadness and even anger, but most times with the assurance that I am keeping the promise I made to Larry even as I create new chapters in my life.

I have come to the realization that I honor his life by moving on with mine. At the same time, I know that I have more "promises to keep and miles to go before I sleep" on this journey. In some ways marking this anniversary makes tomorrow feel like a new beginning, perhaps a little the way a freshman in high school or college, having survived that first year, feels more experienced and equipped to handle what may come. I am certain there are many more lessons to be learned, many more tests to be endured, many more slips and slides that will make me cringe and doubt my ability to persevere. But comfort comes from knowing Larry has kept his promise to be here with me every step of the way. I hear his laughter and feel his presence, as well as his concern, with each decision I make. And with that in mind I look back on a year that has gone by with excruciating slowness, and yet. . . .

Wasn't it just yesterday that he was here?

Three hundred sixty-five days gone?

Without him?

On my own?

I think of the need to constantly fill the gaping holes in my daily routine, times when I would have been doing something with or for Larry such as going to doctor appointments, picking up meds, setting up social dates, working on the newsletter for his volunteer work, talking, laughing—even arguing. Hours and hours every day that without him are suddenly empty and without some definable purpose.

When we had the adult daycare business, I wrote books for caregivers in which I counseled them to prepare themselves for the day when the almost 24/7 tasks of giving care to a loved one would end, and they would need to fill those hours with other activities and tasks. And here I am, just a year in, still facing far too many days when the best I can do is figure out how to get from rising in the morning to going to bed at night.

That undercurrent of disbelief lingered all this past year. There are still days when I am in the middle of something and I simply cannot believe that he is never coming back. I have met this in a variety of ways. I have been angry at what is to me the injustice of it all. Why him? At times I have been defeated by the demanding work of facing a future without him, unable to fathom how I might maintain this can-do spirit he counted on me having. But the truth is, on most of those days, my belief that he is here in spirit to guide me, keeps me strong. I often find myself thinking, "What would Larry say to me right now?"

I watch a lot of home and garden television these days, and frequently am moved to take on some renovation project. So much of the condo we shared seems useless these days. There are entire rooms I simply pass through without ever occupying the space. The loft that used to serve as my home office has been abandoned as I started using Larry's desk in our bedroom. It occurs to me that I am also restructuring me, although I am ill-equipped to sustain what for me is the challenging work of making plans, reaching out, maintaining connections. At the same time, I face this feeling that I have lost my identity. Who is the stranger staring back at me from the mirror each morning?

I doubt I will ever again have someone in my life—meaning romance or marriage. Do I even want that? Do I want to go through the effort it will take to know someone on that level? To have someone know me? Then there is the ongoing confusion about how I am supposed to feel—am I grieving appropriately? enough? There was always a bit of survivor guilt going on, and it does linger. Why him and not me, who rarely plays by the rules, especially those associated with personal health and preventive care?

I do see progress. Buying the place in Florida felt incredibly right. Then there is the fact that I continue to work—the ability to lose myself in the stories and characters for hours each day is both a surprise and a blessing. That realization gives me hope for the future. I love writing stories, especially doing research. The process fills many of those lonely hours. And, of course, there are the connections with others. The friendships that blossomed where they had been only buds before.

And yet, underlying any progress is how to explain to others who I know only want to know that I am okay, that although I am doing fine, I am still a work in progress, and what is "fine" today may have shattered by tomorrow. A pronouncement of some plan or intent made today may be taken back tomorrow or next week. I begin to understand Larry's decision to refuse to discuss his health. It must have been so frustrating to try and explain that any description of his condition was relative at best. There were degrees, and there was never the possibility of fulfilling the hope he must have seen spring to the eyes of friends and family—and me—when he admitted to feeling better.

I suspect that as time goes on my need to record what I am experiencing will be ever less prolific. But I will continue, hoping my experiences and ramblings help me find a path through it all and perhaps afford some measure of hope and comfort for others. After a year, I see that the common denominator is that each piece of this in its own way cements the message: *You can do this. More to the point: You* must *do this.*

MAY–WEEK ONE OF YEAR TWO

A great deal has been written about survival of the first year but extraordinarily little about what happens after that milestone has passed. Other people in my shoes but a little farther down the grief trail have agreed that this is not a journey with an end or destination in sight. This is a rough road with curves and turns and bumps and no real finish line.

I have just returned from what a friend referred to as my "vision quest"—a week alone in beautiful Door County Wisconsin. For those not familiar with the geography: when you look at a map of Wisconsin, Door County is the thumb that sticks out in the upper right. It is the Cape Cod of the Midwest—charming, quaint, picturesque. I planned this trip last August as I began to look ahead to this one-year anniversary. A mere four months into my first year as a widow I decided that I would take a trip once that year ended. It would not be intended as a vacation or sightseeing trip but rather as a kind of sabbatical. It would not only be a week to remember and reflect, but also a week to take stock and look ahead.

I set out midweek. The sky is blue, and the sun is out, both signs that seem to bode well for the adventure I am beginning. I know the way but am curious to see if the GPS will take a different route—and it does. The trip itself is about three hours but I miss a detour and spend an extra half-hour roaming up and down side roads trying to find my way. Where under normal circumstances I might feel frustrated I realize that what I am feeling is a little giddy. Getting a bit lost marks this as an adventure. I pass

May

freshly plowed fields and because the temperature here has risen to the low seventies, I open my windows and the moon roof of the car and breathe in the farm smells—*all* of them! There are cows tending their calves and the parallel tracks of freshly plowed and seeded fields. What I observe is rebirth. What I think is, "Starting over."

The detour takes me a good way up the center of the peninsula instead of along the shores of Green Bay. On this route I pass forests speckled with the white petals of trillium and occasionally the sunshine yellow of a marsh marigold. Eventually I wind my way to the shore on the bay side and follow the road through the quaint villages of Ephraim, Sister Bay, Ellison Bay and on to my destination at the very tip—Gills Rock. I stop for the perishables that will supplement the food I brought with me.

The cottage I've rented is well marked and rests just where the main road turns east toward Lake Michigan and the other side of the peninsula. It is mid-afternoon as I unlock the door after finding the key in a clay flowerpot on the porch steps. I unpack the car and settle in. The main room looks out onto the rock-strewn beach and the bay. Two white pelicans with their orange beaks are cruising by as gulls shriek at them from above. On the beach are two Adirondack chairs and a fire pit. Discovering I don't have enough "bars" for my cell phone to work, I count that as confirmation that this is a time for minimizing electronics and just *being*. The sunset is glorious, followed by a beautiful crescent moon that spotlights the water. I fall asleep a little excited about what the week might bring.

The following day I take a ferry over to Washington Island. In contrast to the mainland, the island feels deserted. I have the road to myself as I drive to the Sievers Fiber School where they hold workshops in fiber arts during the season. After a lovely conversation with some of the staff there, I move on to the Stavkirke, a replica of a medieval Norwegian church style that focuses on the use of vertical posts. It is a quiet peaceful respite with a prayer path through the meadow and woods surrounding it. I spend some time there thinking back over this last year—how fast the time has passed; how impossible it is to believe that Larry is gone. I drive back to the docks for a late lunch at a Danish bakery and cafe before catching the ferry.

Back at the cottage I spend a couple of hours working on my latest novel then decide to clean out the winter waste from the large flower bed in the front yard. This is certainly not something I was asked to do, but it feels so good to do this physical work and uncover the beginnings of the perennials that in another month will fill the space. Another lovely sunset I enjoy as I eat my supper of bread, cheese, and fruit, and I am ready for what tomorrow might bring.

The next day dawns cool and cloudy as I drive to the other side of the peninsula to hike in a state park along the shores of Lake Michigan. I am the only person there, as will often be the case this week. In a month the roads and shops and parks will be crowded, but I have come at the best time for the solitude and reflection I need. Unfortunately, on this nature walk, I am finally driven away by the swarms of May flies that hatch during this time. They don't bite but they are a nuisance. I drive back to the bay side and down to the village of Ephraim for a cherry pancake breakfast at a favorite place Larry and I never missed. It's comforting to find these familiar places still operating.

As I eat, I am able to get cell phone service only to retrieve a message from my dermatologist to call in. I have a long history of pre-cancerous and squamous cell skin lesions, and I pretty much know when something is going to need treatment. The doctor

May

and I finally connect later that evening using the cottage's land line. As I suspected, a spot on my leg biopsied before I left for this trip north needs surgery, and while there is no urgency and certainly no need to abandon my plans for the week, the whole thing is unsettling as once again I face facts: clearly there will be bumps in the road of my idyllic time here as real life intrudes.

On Saturday I discover the community rummage sale in Sister Bay—this is a one-day sale with a map to the houses. As I drive from sale to sale, I discover parts of the area I would not normally see—neighborhoods and back roads and narrow country lanes. From there I drive down the shore through all the little towns (including Fish Creek and Egg Harbor south of Ephraim) to a gallery in a refurbished barn that is hosting a Shepherd's Market— a gathering of weavers and spinners and llama farmers offering demonstrations of their craft and skeins of wonderful hand-dyed yarn. I am at best a novice knitter and weaver but cannot resist buying some. And because spontaneity has become the watch word for this week, I sign up for a papermaking workshop for Sunday afternoon.

Sunday is another amazing day that begins with attending services at the local Unitarian church. During the service a woman reads aloud *Oh, The Places You'll Go* by Dr. Seuss. She had chosen the book because of the graduation season, but it really speaks to me as I recall how many times Larry would ask me what I planned to do after he died. He was so insistent that I must spread my wings and go places and do things and leave myself open to adventures. After the service I tell the reader how much the story touched me, and she gives me her copy of the book.

Once again, the kindness of strangers touches my heart.

The papermaking workshop is another delightful time. The process is fascinating, the instructor patient and kind; the others in the class easy to be with. Each event of the day puts a smile on my face and a calmness in my soul that has been missing since my return from Florida.

Monday I am awakened by thunder before sunrise, and, as I stand at the window with my coffee after the storm passes, I see some commercial fisherman preparing to go out for the morning. I take a long walk, relieved to discover the rain seems to have sent the May flies back into hiding. When I return mid-morning, I see another fishing boat pulling into the dock and watch the men unload their catch.

Because the rain is predicted to continue off and on through the day, I go to some of the galleries that Larry and I always enjoyed. He so appreciated the talents of others and marveled at their creativity. I have brought along the materials for creating blank books for cancer patients at a hospital in Milwaukee. I need some paper to finish them, so I stop at a framing and art supply shop. While they do not have the paper, they give me two garbage bags filled with the cuttings from their mats after framing. Back at the cottage I spend the rest of the afternoon creating new journal covers and thinking how very benevolent people are if you open the door to them. Of course, that's the lesson Larry tried to instill all along.

On Tuesday I decide that even though I had planned to stay a full week, I am ready to go home. The only reason to stay would be that I had scheduled it that way. But I realize that I am done with schedules, and I pack up the car and head south. I stop for a final meal at a Swedish restaurant that we enjoyed often with friends. When I arrive home the lilac bushes lining the entrance to the complex are in full bloom, a sure message from Larry to me. I feel lighter and less encumbered by all the "shoulds" society teaches for those grieving. I left those behind early in the week and hopefully they have not followed me back.

May

I am ready to move on into another year knowing there will be sad times, times when I am furious at the hand Larry and I were dealt. But then I will remember that we had 42 years that were filled to overflowing with memories and laughter and crises averted and crises met with grace and dignity.

And I will go on . . .

I see now that the challenges we faced and the arguments we had were detours and construction zones as we found our way down unknown roads and byways until once again our paths merged and we embraced, breathless with relief at still being together.

In short, for over four decades he loved me, and I loved him. We were each other's best friend and trusted counselor, and the fruit of that love story will sustain me for whatever time I have left in this world. Yes, I will cry, and I will sometimes rant. We all want more of something so right. But in my heart, I know that what we shared is far beyond what many people get.

And after a year, I finally face the hard truth: I am a widow.

I understand that even so I will always shudder every time I even think of that word, much less speak it aloud or mark its check box on some form.

But I am now and ever shall be a woman who was half of an incomparable love story. In that I am truly blessed—and with that always in mind I begin year two.

June

Lately it seems as if there's been an unusual rash of health challenges for my friends—a recurring malignant brain tumor, a stroke, three separate incidents of heart problems requiring stents and resulting in blood clots and other complications. Is this what growing old is about?

Yuck!

I think about the years that Larry struggled to fight back from his stroke, the heart issues, his brain tumor that was no less destructive simply because it was benign, and finally the lung diseases that partnered to take his life. And I realize that knowing what I now know about the best laid fights of man against disease, in far too many situations the disease eventually wins. I am afraid for my friends and for their spouses and their children and grandchildren. And I feel so very helpless to do more than simply let them know that I am here for them.

There is a saying "What you leave behind is not what is engraved in stone monuments, but what is woven into the lives of others." (Pericles)

I am tempted to admit defeat, to say that it's all downhill from here. But I know that Larry would be furious with that path. He had that gift of reaching out to others, listening, and applauding and sympathizing and laughing or crying with them. He celebrated the successes and milestones of those around him, and he consoled them when there were those moments that did not go as planned. He was the proverbial glass-half-full person and even now more than a year after his death, he is intricately woven into the fiber of those friends who witnessed his years of struggle and now hope to be equally as courageous and strong and giving as they face challenges of their own.

So, what I try to practice every day is that same spirit of focus-on-you-not-me. I feel I not only want to do this because it makes me a calmer, more peaceful person, but I also feel called to be that poor substitute for what these dear friends once received from Larry. It is a daily struggle for I am by nature far more self-centered than he ever was. But the rewards are so great that every day giving of myself to others becomes a little easier, a little more normal, and a great deal more rewarding.

July

Well, last 4th of July I went to a party at the home of dear friends and came close to having a weeping meltdown in front of everyone. So understandably this year when I had invitations to not one but two parties, I was more than a little nervous. The one thing I have learned is that even the best of friends is ready for me to move on now that we have all reached that one-year marker. I am tempted to take the easy way out, fake illness and not go to either party, but I know Larry would be disappointed in such cowardice. With that in mind, I see no option but to accept both invitations.

The first party on the 3rd causes special concern. This annual event was not held last year because the hosts were traveling so as I prepare to go this year, I realize that this will be a large gathering with several people that I have known for years but who are more acquaintances than close friends. All of them will know of Larry's death, and many of them will be seeing me for the first time since the memorial service.

So, I go.

And I have a lovely evening!

I realize there is something to be said for others assuming one year is the tipping point for ending grief. Oh, they understand the sadness will always be there, but their expectation that life goes on eases the moment. There are only a few somber inquiries on how I am doing, and for the most part, any conversation about Larry has to do with some memory that makes everyone smile or laugh out loud. The purchase of a second home certainly helps—giving everyone something to talk about other than the fact Larry is, for the first time, not at this gathering. Overall, there is the assumption that I have made it through year one and am doing just fine.

Buoyed by that success I arrive at the party on the 4th. This is a much smaller gathering with some fresh faces there as there were last year when I made my sudden exit. This time I find that I am able to meet people without worrying. Some know of Larry's death, and, for those who do not I am able to say without hesitation "my late husband" or "my husband who died last year" and let the conversation continue naturally. So, on both scores I count that as growth on my part. I have moved past the it's-all-about-me-and-my-grief stage to the one-day-at-a-time stage. That said, the more time that passes with others getting back to their lives, the more pervasive and devastating my personal loneliness becomes.

What remains true is that *if* those connections are to be part of my routine, it will be up to me to tend them—to be the one who makes the first move or offers the invitation. That's a huge problem because I don't like to bother or insert myself into the already busy lives of my friends, so for now I am trying to find things to do on my own that at least put me in the company of others—even strangers. Someone told me about a sketching class at the local recreation department, so I signed up for that, and I also signed up to volunteer for the annual film festival in September. The class was fine although no lasting connections resulted. The film festival is yet to be determined.

So, it goes. Hour by hour, day by day until like the July 4th parties of last year and this, I realize that I have changed and grown and coped.

JULY CONTINUES

As encouraging as Larry was at the possibility of my re-inventing myself, I had serious reservations. Now as I move more deeply into year two of widowhood, I find that re-invention is not only a possibility, but also in so many ways a necessity.

As mentioned before, the further removed from Larry's actual death I get, the more I feel overwhelmed by the loneliness and the sheer number of hours I spend by myself. I have a tendency as well as a genetic predisposition toward depression. So, before that becomes an issue to be acknowledged and fought, I am determined to take a good hard look at the realities of my life. Larry worried that given my normal reclusive personality, I would falter. He actually called friends and asked them to care for me in various ways—remind me to pay the quarterly taxes, invite me to join them to watch a game or see a play or movie. At first, others were religious about following through, but as time passed? Not so much.

I have at least a couple of ways to digest this: I can choose to be sad and hurt and feel sorry for myself; or I can understand that there is no negative intent. My friends still love me and if I made the first move, they would definitely say "yes."

So, it seems to me that the answer is to expand my network, something I had begun to do even before Larry died. For all our married life we were part of this close-knit community of friends, rarely seeing the need to branch out and explore other possibilities. I am beginning to accept the need for me to widen the circle, and over this last year I have worked hard at that. These days I often work on my writing in coffeehouses surrounded by people, and I regularly attend a summer music series on Sunday mornings. I have resumed my involvement in two book discussion groups and continue to attend services and work on committees within my faith. But in any of those cases am I really connecting with people beyond the moment? They are there, and I am there, but after and in between...?

After Larry died, I decided to give up my little writing studio once the lease ran out last summer. I still feel that was the right move at the time. But today as I was writing at a local coffeehouse, it seemed a promising idea to find some place where I would be seeing some of the same people each time I went there. Doing that, I might connect with these people on a deeper level. Down the street from the coffeehouse is an art co-op. These are painters and weavers and photographers sharing a large loft space. I stopped in and spoke with three members of the co-op who told me about a small available space. On Saturday I will meet the co-op manager and see what we can work out. I feel good about this. While it doesn't completely resolve the issue of loneliness, I feel that it has the potential to be a place where I might find a new direction in my constant battle against isolation.

JULY–COMING TO AN END
Once again, the time has come for the annual visit to Madison for a special weekend. Larry always chose the weekend that the shops along State Street were holding their mid-summer Maxwell Street days. I would shop for bargains; we would have dinner in

a lovely restaurant then see a play. On Saturday we would wander through the incredible Farmer's Market on the Square—a mile-long wonderland of organic fruits and veggies, baked goods, plants and flowers and soapbox orators speaking out about this or that topic of the day. Later we would go to the wonderful Memorial Union Terrace overlooking Lake Mendota and watch sailboats while we ate huge cones of ice cream made right there on campus. Before heading for home, we would take a walk along the lake path that runs from the Union past dorms and other campus buildings along the shore of the lake, and he would tell stories of his days on campus.

Last year I went there for a writing workshop, and as part of that visit placed some of Larry's ashes along the lake path down near the water and near the dorm he lived in as a student there. This year when I walked the path I stopped to "visit" that spot and restore what remains of the rocks I had stacked there last year. I suspect by next year erosion will have entirely swept the memorial away, but for me, it will always be there.

I shopped at the farmer's market and the Maxwell Street sales and while I did not see a play, I did sit on the Union terrace listening to live music while I enjoyed the ice cream. When I started for home yesterday, I felt so peaceful and light-hearted and very much as if I had shared this time with Larry.

About 20 miles outside Madison, it started to sprinkle even though the sun was out. And then I saw this rainbow or rather half a rainbow. But size aside, it was the best rainbow I have ever seen. It was so close that I could clearly see every color band and it stayed there riding along with me for another 20 miles or so.

By now it's obvious that I am a person who believes in signs—I believe they are all around us if we will simply open hearts and minds to discovering and receiving them. I have no doubt at all that this rainbow that came literally out of the blue was Larry letting me know that he agreed.

It had been a lovely weekend.

August

In year one there were, of course, a lot of "firsts" that had to be navigated and braved. I am here to report they do continue, fewer now but still there. And still a painful reminder that this going forward step by step and change after change is my new reality. Bottom line? There is no magic in that one-year anniversary.

Today, for the first time, I went to a matinee movie *by myself*. It was a drizzly Sunday afternoon with back-to-school coolness in the air and overcast skies. A movie I had wanted to see was playing at the local theater. Given the history of friends turning back to what is routine for them and my reluctance to intrude on that, I realized that pretty much everyone I might have invited to see the film with me had already been there and done that. So, I had some choices: I could wait for it to come out on one of the many streaming services and watch it at home; I could seek out some less likely candidates to see it with me; or I could go by myself.

I wanted to see this movie so ruled out #1 since at the time I did not have any subscriptions. I have not made much progress in making the first moves to include myself in the activities that Larry and I used to take for granted as a couple so that ruled out #2. That left #3 which seemed to be the logical choice since I have had a gift card for the theater sitting on the kitchen table for several months. So, I went and totally enjoyed the film. I left knowing not only could I do this but that I *would* do this more often.

The journey continues . . .

AUGUST–ANOTHER SPECIAL TRIP
This time, I spent a few lovely late summer days with friends in the lake country of northern Wisconsin. Larry and I made many happy memories up there—hiking, fishing, and, of course, eating! I had not gone fishing since his death but found it is a little like riding a bike—it all comes back. Larry used to tease me about my side-arm method of casting, and he was clearly stunned, but impressed when I wasn't the least bit squeamish about putting live bait on the hook myself. His favorite photo of me was from the time I caught a sizable, small-mouthed bass from the pier of our friends' cottage.

One afternoon I sat alone on that pier while my friends went off in the boat to fish. I thought about all the wonderful times Larry and I shared, all the ideas for stories that were developed as we sat together or hiked through the woods in the fall, all the plans we made for our future. I find that at moments like these I am not saddened but rather I am grateful.

I had such joy (and yes, sometimes the frustration) of life with this man. And every day that he is gone I appreciate more fully how carefully he prepared me for the life I would need to build without him. It is not always easy but sure beats the alternative of wallowing in self-pity.

September

A few days ago, it occurred to me that for those of us whose life partner suffered a long and often painful end, perhaps months or as in my case—and perhaps yours—years, there is one small compensation in living on: I realized that I no longer worry all the time or walk through my days waiting for some catastrophe. I no longer sleep with one ear open for a possible change in breathing or a fall or other calamity. Not that I wouldn't cut off a vital body part to have him back for an hour or a day, but there is that release of responsibility.

I was basking in this freedom from worry and stress when a couple of days later, I developed what my doctor later referred to as "a-typical" symptoms that lasted through one night and into the morning. Ingrained with a history of managing things on my own, I told myself the choice was to either sit and worry and hope symptoms that had lasted several hours would simply go away or get myself to the walk-in clinic I went to when I had a similar fright last year.

Foolishly I drove myself to the clinic where I found that my description of what was going on was taken *very* seriously. I was told to go directly from there to the Urgent Care clinic near a hospital, and, once there, the clinic doctor gave me her choice: either go in an ambulance or call someone to come and take me, but either way, in her opinion, I needed hospitalization immediately.

I called Larry's sister, and long story short, I was in the hospital for two nights and three days. They ran tests, drew blood every four hours, scheduled a stress test, connected me to monitors that limited my movement while at the same time encouraging me to walk the halls, and eventually sent me home without really identifying the root of the problem. I came away with a solid baseline of test results that told me whatever my problem was it was not a cardiac issue. That certainly was good news given a long family history of heart disease.

One of my many shortcomings is that once I learn I am no longer at risk, I move on. I have no curiosity for demanding answers to questions that are still open-ended.

Of course, the real bonus in this rather unsettling episode was that, as news spread of my hospitalization, friends came and kept coming and calling and checking in. Mentally I knew that I could have called any one of them at the first sign of trouble (and they were plenty upset that I didn't!), but emotionally I had not yet accepted that their need to be there for me was more than being there because Larry had asked them to be. I had not yet accepted that they wanted to be there because it was *me*.

October

Today I was walking with my friend along the downtown shores of Lake Michigan, and while, as mentioned before, this time of year is not my favorite, the day was spectacular. Calm sparkling water, a few boats heading out for a last run, the park dotted with trees dressed in the palette of autumn. As usual, my friend and I tackled a wide span of topics, ranging from local to national news to what was going on with other friends to my upcoming return to Florida where I would be in residence in the condo I had bought last spring.

Somewhere in there I mentioned that when I returned from this season in Florida, I was thinking of selling the condo Larry and I shared in a northern suburb of Milwaukee and renting a place downtown. We had always wanted to live downtown, closer to the venues and restaurants and parks we enjoyed. Unfortunately, his compromised lungs and the uncertainty of air quality in city living made that unrealistic.

The "W" Word

But there is nothing wrong with my lungs, and because I am feeling increasingly restless and isolated in the suburban setting. I'd been thinking of making that change. I would not only be in walking distance of the lake and the fabulous art museum and other places I enjoyed, but I would also be closer to this friend. She and her husband live in a historic landmark building that is part condominium and part rental, and she immediately urged me to investigate renting there right away.

I laughed and reminded her I was talking spring, but she was not to be dissuaded. She told me I at least needed to get on the waiting list for an opening, and our walk ended in a visit to the office to sign me up. To our surprise there was no waiting list. The manager handed us the keys to a vacant apartment so I could see what it was like. We took the elevator up and I unlocked the door to a corner unit, still laughing at the ridiculousness of looking at anything now.

And then I walked inside.

I am not sure what it is with me and light-filled historic places, but that feeling I had when I walked into that first place in Sarasota, was back. Sunlight poured through large windows on two sides of the spacious living room revealing a panoramic view of the park across the street and the lake beyond that. There were wonderful vintage details like lofty ceilings, crown moldings and parquet wooden floors. My friend stood back and watched me discover the small kitchen and bath, both of which some people would have wanted to gut, but that I saw as charming. The place was straight out of a novel set in early 20th century NYC.

"It's perfect," I said.

"So?"

I laughed. "I leave for Florida in less than a month. How can I possibly get the condo ready to list and get moved in such a short time?"

My friend saw no problem. "Think about it," she advised. "You can do this."

A sleepless night. A lot of pacing through my condo, already subconsciously dividing stuff into take-donate-sell piles; sitting at the dining room table, drawing rough floor plans as I arranged my furniture in the new apartment; checking listings of currently for-sale units in my community to get comps. I spent long hours going through the finances, trying to look at the numbers and ask hard questions as Larry would have. What if the condo took a long time to sell? What if I had to take it off the market and list it again in spring? What was I thinking, signing a rental lease and then leaving it vacant for the five months I was in Florida?

It felt insane.

And yet it felt so right.

Next morning, I called my tax accountant and financial advisor and laid out the details. Both were surprised to hear about yet another real estate transaction barely six months after my venture in Florida but assured me I would be okay either way—stay put or move. I drove back downtown and returned to the rental office. I asked if I could look at the place again—alone. This time I sat on the floor of the empty apartment and tried to imagine my life there. I closed my eyes and absorbed the sounds of city living—traffic, a siren, voices in the corridor outside the apartment. *Life!* I talked to Larry, working through the logistics as I wandered from the living room to the kitchen to the bedroom and back again. I mentally went through all the pros and cons, but somewhere deep inside I understood I was going to do this. I understood that this, as much as the change I had made in Florida, was yet another step to building a life without him.

I returned to the office and completed the paperwork for the lease, then drove home and called the realtor I knew lived in my condo community and had sold several units there. By week's end the place was listed; I had sorted through years of stuff and scheduled an "estate sale," and I had completed the lease signing and received the keys to the apartment. Needless to say, my friend was delighted.

Now began daily trips to and from to move the smaller things, fill the kitchen and bathroom cabinets, transport clothing and linens and find them new homes in the limited storage space there. I scheduled movers and staged the condo with the furnishings left to be sold in the estate sale in December, praying by then I would have a viable offer. I told friends and family of the new plan, and was not at all surprised at their reactions:

"But you just bought...."

"What if you don't like it?"

And always, the standard: "It really hasn't been that long, Jo. Maybe...."

I watched as they mentally calculated the costs of rent and condo fees in two places—at least until the Wisconsin condo sold. But I was way ahead of them, having done all that.

The truth is I'm a bit weird in that I *like* to move. I like weeding through pieces of the past and imagining a new future. I like arranging my favorite things against a new background. And once I set my sights on a plan, it's full steam ahead pretty much 24/7 until the end result is achieved. So, while I had had doubts about not having enough time to get everything done, once I set things in motion, I couldn't stop until it was all in place. This was different from buying the condo in Florida. This would truly be "home," a fresh start for me on so many levels. I began to appreciate the therapeutic advantages of taking this on. I had no time to grieve, be lonely, or feel sorry for myself. Every moment of every day was packed.

I thought of Larry constantly: what would he say? What would he advise? But never in a sad or mournful way. I knew he was right there, enjoying this new adventure with me.

Thanksgiving

Back in Florida. Head spinning as I come to grips with the huge changes in my life over the last several months. I was barely in the apartment in downtown Milwaukee before it was time to head south. And here I am in my own place as well. In both places the pictures are hung and the closets filled. Here in Sarasota, that all happened in spring, and I have returned to a place that feels like mine, surrounded by carefully chosen items that reflect the life Larry and I shared here even when we lived in the rental unit. When I return to Wisconsin in spring, the apartment will also be fully organized. I find a good deal of comfort in having things in their place, although do not for one minute get the idea that I am a "neat freak." The spaces I occupy are often filled with piles of papers and files and just plain stuff to the point where periodically I go on a tear and re-organize everything.

The cloud hanging over all this euphoria is that there has been no offer on my Wisconsin condo, but clearly, I have much to be thankful for today, and I will savor that with a walk on the beach followed later by a traditional turkey dinner with my friends down here. I will miss preparing the dinner myself, instead bringing my assigned contribution of a fruit plate to the gathering. But the blessings of being with others who knew Larry and loved him and will share memories of him as naturally as they might talk about someone actually at the table far outweigh any opportunity to try a new recipe for stuffing or pie.

DECEMBER–HAPPY HOLIDAYS FOR ME!
An offer! Some back and forth, and then: SOLD!
What a relief!
Today I am starting to gather the information my accountant will need for preparing my taxes. Oh, how Larry must be laughing at the very idea of me gathering financial documents for this annual process. He and I always understood one of the secrets of our happy marriage was that from day one we kept parts of our finances separate—no joint bank accounts and no shared credit cards. When tax preparation time came, I was always the one who kept my receipts and such literally in a shoebox. When he called for an accounting of my writing business and donations and other tax items he needed, I would dump the box on the dining room table and spend several hours sorting through and organizing as I calculated sums for the form he'd created for me.

And then there are the holidays to tackle. This year I feel more like getting into the spirit of things, as I plan to resurrect the traditional Christmas Day brunch we always hosted. I am learning that adding new adventures to old traditions might just be the best way through this thing called grieving. Remembering who I am, where I came from, how I've changed and adapted even before Larry died is a key piece of figuring out who I am now and will be going forward.

I do know that some of the actions I've taken have given me the confidence I needed to overcome the fear and anxiety of believing I didn't know how to do this. And the truth is I'm pretty much making it up as I go. My friends interact with me in a different way now. There are a fair number of stunned looks that I interpret as "Who are you and what have you done with the Jo we thought we knew?" Admittedly I get a bit of a kick out of their surprise and shock. While they have always seen me as someone who marched to my own drumbeat, they also saw me as one half of a pair where Larry led the way—where I never questioned him leading the way. Now I am a solo act, and others seem eager to learn what I might do next.

December

Living in a condo I had never shared with him may have helped. Certainly, sharing part of it with family and friends was a major plus. Early in our marriage we often were apart for those holidays—me with family in Virginia while Larry stayed in Wisconsin for work. It was after my parents died in the 90's and we sold the adult daycare business that we began our own holiday traditions. One that he enjoyed was our annual car ride through neighborhoods to look at decorations. We would put a holiday CD in the car player and sing along as we made the tour. This year I decided to revive that and immediately realized there were two big problems: 1) a lot of houses are dark because "snowbirds" have yet to return; and 2) without Larry there to sing along, the evening felt forced.

Lesson learned: Not everything will work. I thought keeping this tradition would add to my holiday celebration.

It didn't.

I can't re-create the past.

I can only move forward.

NEW YEAR'S EVE
Like many people, for me New Year's Eve is a time of celebration, reflection and anticipation. I've just come from a party given by friends with wonderful food and fellowship to kick off another year. After changing into my "jammies," I sit outside on my balcony and, although I can't see them, listen to the fireworks. I light a candle and take stock of the year just passed. Certainly, it was a year of change for me. I bought a second home here in Florida; I sold a home in Wisconsin and became a renter; I moved from the 'burbs to the city. I continue working, meeting deadlines, and writing stories that help me find my way through my own challenges.

What might this new year bring?

I think I might finally be ready to travel. Tomorrow I will start researching possible trips to Europe. Larry and I always wanted to go to Normandy.

Yeah, Normandy sounds exactly right.

January–March

Time does slip away, and I take it as a healthy sign that during this time, I have had little to report and little need to vent or use journaling as a tool for figuring out my life. I have almost made it through the first two years, and along the way I have made some huge changes and dealt with some major challenges—bought and sold a condo; rented a place in the city; weathered a couple of health scares; and, most of all, continued to press on as I find my way. Now I have finally arrived at the place Larry and I spoke about so often—I will travel abroad and see some of the places we planned to see. And I go with the assurance that he travels with me in spirit.

Normandy—here I come.

April

The flight from Chicago to Paris is uneventful. I sleep despite my excitement—and nervousness—at striking out on this new adventure. Everything seems to be going smoothly until we land and I discover my luggage did not land with me. I file the paperwork and the agent gives me a form to submit to be reimbursed for whatever I need to buy between now and when they find and deliver my bag (hopefully within forty-eight hours).

I meet our guide for the trip and with a few other members of our group, travel by bus from Paris to the quaint village of Honfleur. Frankly I am underwhelmed by the two others on the bus, fearing they might be indicative of the rest of the group. One woman seems eager to make it clear she is a seasoned traveler and knows a great deal about all we are to experience. Another, whose luggage is also MIA is inconsolable. One would think she had lost her child rather than a mere suitcase. I find I struggle more these days with those who face a situation that "is what it is" and refuse to stop whining. Fortunately, our guide is a no-nonsense Dutch woman who promises to be unruffled by anyone or anything.

Once we reach the hotel, while others go off to their rooms to unpack, she gives me directions to the town's lone department store, and I set out.

The store's selection is not exactly Macy's—more suitable for the 20-somethings who shop at stores like Urban Outfitters, but at this point I literally have the clothes (down to the undergarments) I'm wearing. With travel from Milwaukee to Chicago and then several hours on the plane, they are more than a little ripe. After an exhaustive search, I finally come away with two tops and a skirt that look like I can wash them (along with the trousers I'm wearing) in the sink and a couple of undergarments that are as far as this old lady can get from Victoria Secret knockoffs.

Back at the hotel, I shower and change, wash out my cast-offs and drape them over the towel bars to dry, then head downstairs for the welcome reception. This tour is organized by a company that does tours for alumni groups at major universities. The small college I attended in Tennessee is definitely not on their radar, so I signed up for the trip using my connections as a longtime season ticket holder for Marquette University's men's basketball team. That turns out to be a plus, because when I introduce myself to the others and admit I really have no direct alumni connections, that and the missing luggage open a door, and I find myself surrounded by some who share my devotion to the basketball team and others who seem to be fascinated by my this-too-shall-pass attitude regarding the missing luggage. As the group heads out to a local waterside restaurant for dinner, I feel more connected and realize my earlier concerns have quickly been laid to rest. Later as

I prepare for bed, I look out to see a large river cruise boat docking for the night and I smile.

"We're in Normandy, my honey," I exclaim as I dance around the room with the photo of Larry I always have on my bedside table.

NORMANDY–DAY 2

We begin the day with a full breakfast in the hotel dining room. Long ago a writer friend who often attended the same conferences I did, had made a point of letting me know she would seek out others to dine with to take advantage of getting to know new people. She hoped I would not be offended. I thought the plan was brilliant and in preparing for this trip I had decided I would make a point of sitting with different people at each meal until I get to know everyone in the group. I have dressed in a blend of new clothes and washed-and-dried airplane clothes, and several people inquire sympathetically about the status of my luggage. I dismiss their concerns, reminding them I kind of have a license to shop so really don't see a problem.

The morning activity is a walking tour of Honfleur, so we all don our "whisperers"—battery-powered listening devices that allow our guide to speak in a normal voice. Normally I cringe at the very thought of organized tours, but quickly realize this is the perfect way to become acclimated to this charming town where not only do I not know my way, but do not speak the language. Knowing that we have the afternoon free after lunch, I pay close attention to streets and places I might want to explore in depth later. Every step I take makes me think of how Larry would love this. I take a bazillion photos and recall a time when we were in London and Larry teased me about how many pictures I took of the Changing of the Guard on our first day there.

After enjoying lunch with the group, I set out on my own, exploring the side streets and period architecture. I see a couple of For Sale signs and momentarily daydream about what it might be like to live here. I can practically hear Larry protesting: "Enough!"

My afternoon ends a local grocery store where I buy some fruit and cheese to have in my room for dinner. We're on our own for that meal and a couple of people invited me to join them, but I decide to take time to take a nap and catch up on my journal before heading down to hear the evening's lecture on the history of D-Day.

The speaker (and our expert leader for tomorrow's tour) is a British man who has lived in Normandy for over twenty-five years. Our guide tells me his wife died some months ago and this is his first tour since then. My heart goes out to him, and I hope doing work he loves will be as therapeutic for him as writing is for me.

NORMANDY–DAY 3

After another filling breakfast, we board the bus for what promises to be a very full day. I am a history buff and am especially interested in World War II history so am very much looking forward to what may come. Michael, our leader, is in top form channeling everyone from Eisenhower to Churchill to Roosevelt as he entertains us with stories from Omaha Beach to the Calvados coastline to the US Military Cemetery to the abandoned German bunkers and unfinished gun turrets at Pointe du Hoc. I cannot look around or mentally record information fast enough. My mind reels with possible story scenarios.

That said, I am deeply disappointed with the cemetery—an iconic place I had so looked forward to visiting. There are flocks of tourists everywhere, all wearing their devices as their guides speak aloud the history of the setting. I want silence. I want reverence and awe as I stare across row after row of white crosses and Stars of David. I wander as far as I dare from our group and the others, seeking, but not really finding, the moment I had imagined.

Our bus travels down a narrow road, the hedgerows scratching the bus windows, past a stone farmhouse and outbuildings to a German bunker. It strikes me that the French farmer and his wife could see the unsightly trappings of war from their kitchen window. Several yards away, overlooking the Channel, is a large gun on a lazy Susan type platform that was thankfully never finished or put into action. With it the Germans could have mowed down countless Allied soldiers. On this day, it stood rusted and abandoned surrounded by colorful wildflowers that belied the ugliness of its intent.

After parting ways with our guide, the bus ride back to the hotel is quieter. Side conversations or an occasional burst of laughter intersperse the pervasive tranquility as individually we process all that we have learned and seen. I suspect uppermost in most minds is the question of how different our world might be today, had that mission failed. Sometimes I lose sight of just how blessed my life has been, and once again lean into the comfort of silence as I process the wonders of what was and what might have been. I find my thoughts shifting from the distant to the more recent past. In spite of the trials of his many health problems, Larry and I shared over forty years during which we were both present, if not always fully aware, of the gifts we received.

NORMANDY-DAY 4

As if the tour organizers understood how mentally and emotionally exhausting yesterday might be, today we have the entire day free. I spend the morning at the local museum and then shop for holiday gifts for friends and family. Along the way I discover a small shop on a side street where I buy a skirt and shawl to add to my meager wardrobe. My luggage was never put on the plane in Chicago and has now finally arrived in Paris, but for some reason it is being held there. Our group leader is clearly far more concerned than I am. The truth is the missing luggage continues to be a conversation starter that has led to some delightful encounters with others on the trip.

After lunch, I take out the travel-sized watercolor kit I brought along and a sketchpad and head out to indulge my inner-Impressionist. Honfleur was a favorite setting for painters like Claude Monet and his friends. It also was virtually untouched by bombing during the war so there are many locations that invite even an amateur like me to try my hand at sketching and painting. I get so wrapped up in the Zen of painting I am late for dinner and tonight's lecture.

NORMANDY–DAY 5

Another full day ahead as we board the bus and head for Caen and the Peace Memorial Museum. Michael is once again our guide and educates and entertains us with information and stories as we travel. The day is cool and a bit gloomy and I find myself distracted with information overload. Once we leave the museum, we head for Utah Beach where we are left to wander on our own. I walk along the water's edge with no sound except the gentle lapping of the water. I try to imagine what that day must have been like—the noise and the fear and the bloodshed. The beach is barren for the most part—a kind of caramel-colored hard sand. Then I find a perfect scallop shell and although it's probably against some rule, I take it.

Later after lunch, we head for the German cemetery, and to my surprise here I find what I was missing at the cemetery the other day. Almost no one is here. Most of our group has elected to stay inside the small museum building rather than venture out into the misty rain and dampness. I wander the rows of graves marked by simple flat stones and remind myself that here lie sons and husbands and fathers and brothers no less loved than those buried under pristine white markers just a few miles away. These lost souls were labeled as our enemy, and yet I am consumed by sadness and choose to sit alone on the long ride back to Honfleur. Others seem equally lost in thought as they are in what they have seen and heard this day.

At the hotel I am told the hold-up on my luggage is in fact connected to the other woman whose luggage has also been missing. Because she had no identification tags on her bag, they will not send it, and apparently even though my bag is clearly marked, they have decided making two trips is not viable. It strikes me that prior to Larry's death, such blatant unfairness would have upset me to the point that I would not only lose my temper but act out in ways that I find abhorrent—shouting and perhaps even swearing at some innocent who really can do nothing to make the situation better. But in the overall scheme of things, I have learned about what's valuable in life, and a suitcase filled with clothing easily replaced seems so very trivial.

This trip has always been about the adventure, and by definition doesn't an adventure preclude something unexpected? Wasn't a large part of traveling on my own a test to see how I would fare? Traveling to a foreign country in the midst of grief? Spending time with strangers who do not know me and are unlikely to ever really know me? Testing the waters of who me without Larry might become without the pressure of expectations from others who think they know me so well?

I did the right thing, taking on this challenge. In a few short days I have grown and changed, realizing strengths I never could have imagined having. My missing luggage is no more serious than if I were on the highway and missed my exit. My choice would be to panic or to simply keep going until I reached a place where I could safely exit and retrace my route.

I realize our guide is still talking to me about my luggage, telling me she will call this person or that and make sure it arrives before we leave. The dear woman is nearly in tears. I take her hand. "It's just a suitcase," I remind her. "Tell you what. If it does make it before we leave for the airport day after tomorrow, I'll put on a fashion show so everyone can see what they missed."

She laughs, and I realize how much I love that—making someone smile or laugh. Larry was so good at that, and I think maybe I'm getting better.

MAY-YEAR TWO IS IN THE BOOKS
And what a year it has been! Last May, if anyone had told me I would manage complex finances, buy and sell property, move twice, and make a trip to Normandy, I would not have believed any part of that was possible. And yet here I am, happily resettled in my city apartment in Milwaukee, gazing out at Lake Michigan and surrounded by the wonderful memories of a trip that for me was definitely on the Bucket List.

Tomorrow will mark two years since Larry died. I have no special plans for commemorating the day this year other than to take a long walk and then drive past all the places we lived here in Milwaukee, reliving memories attached to each place.

Tonight, I had dinner with friends who told me of their upcoming trip to Ireland. To my delight they urged me to come along.

April

Of course, having just returned from Normandy, the idea seemed ridiculous even though it was clear they were sincere in their invitation to join them. But, over this last year I have discovered that asking "why not?" is a new way to look at opportunities. Certainly, there have been a couple of times when taking that leap has not been the best idea, but far more often, saying yes has led to new adventures and a sense of peace and happiness I had thought I might never know.

Traveling with friends is something I had rejected out of hand. Perhaps this is an opportunity to see how that might go. The trip is still six months away, plenty of time for me to set aside the money needed. I've always wanted to travel to Ireland and the itinerary promises an opportunity to see a good deal of that country. Traveling with two guys eliminates any discussion about possibly sharing a room so I would still have my private space at the end of the day.

Later that night as I am running numbers to be sure of my math—never my strong suit—an email arrives. It's from my friends, sending me the link to the travel company and tour and once again urging me to join them. I lean back and my gaze lands on the photo of Larry I keep on my desk. He's smiling at me with that twinkle in his eye, and I can almost hear him saying, "Why not?"

I click "reply" and type: *I'm in!* before hitting send.

PART THREE
Lessons Learned

And time goes on

I am now more than ten years out from that day when I said goodbye to the love of my life. I have done as Larry asked. I reached out and opened my heart and mind to possibilities. And in doing that, I have found my way to new friendships and self-discovery. I was fortunate that he left a legacy of outlook and behavior that taught me—and others—how to face adversity with grace and dignity.

 I was blessed to have shared a loving relationship with him for forty-plus years. I was privileged to be the beneficiary of his stewardship of our financial security. Neither of us came from wealth, and we certainly did not benefit from some windfall like an inheritance or winning the lottery. But over the years, with careful planning and a cautious approach to spending that sometimes drove me nuts, Larry accumulated the savings that have allowed me to explore this new life without him. I once chastised him about being so thrifty. "We should enjoy life *now*," I said.

He smiled and replied, "The way I see it you're probably going to live to be 105, and I don't want you to run out of money."

How do you argue with that?

The good news is that as the months and years passed, I became more comfortable in the life I had created for myself. The sad news is . . . at least for this memoir, I took a long hiatus from journaling.

I did go to Ireland with my friends, and I did learn I had been right to think traveling on my own in the company of strangers worked best for me. I realized that I am at my core a caregiver and that means when I am with people I know and love, I focus on their needs, their wishes, their comforts. And far too often I do that at the expense of what I want or need.

Over the course of these years, I have traveled with tour groups where I met some interesting people and visited places I had always wanted to see or returned to places I love. I continue to winter in Sarasota but am no longer a property owner there. In both Florida and Wisconsin, I have continued to adjust my living arrangements until now I am comfortably settled in a senior community where many of my basic needs are met. Of course, like nearly everyone who considers moving to such a place, I felt I was far too healthy and much too young. I did it because it seemed the best possible answer to my continued concern about being alone when something happens with my health—and it will. I mostly did it because I knew I was going to move there in a couple of years, so why not get on with it?

Admittedly there are times when I step off the elevator and work my way past a parade of walkers and wheelchairs and I question my choice. But what I have learned is that the appliance does not define the person—nor does the chronological age. I am living in a community of people who have, in most cases, lived fascinating lives and are still deeply engaged in world events today. If there is a secret to their longevity, it is that they care and believe in their ability to continue to be effective and to learn. It is their refusal to allow physical frailties to limit or define them.

They inspire me, and in their midst, I have discovered new ways of coping and thriving.

So, the learning curve continues, and that made me curious to look back over these pages in an attempt to pull out some of the key lessons I learned over those first two years after Larry died. My story is not your story, but in both our stories there are universal truths that have and will sustain us as we continue our journey.

Not everyone gets a Larry

Let's address this right away. Some elements of my journey are unique to me. The marriage Larry and I shared and the relationship we built from the highs and lows of that union is one example.

Other pieces of my journey may resonate with you—or not. Clearly, I am a deeply spiritual person who believes death is not the end and who is constantly on the search for signs that prove that theory. You may find that pure hogwash, or the idea that those who have died live on in some way—even if only in our hearts and minds—may bring you comfort.

And finally, there are the universal truths that connect with every journey to and through coping with the absence of someone who in life was an integral piece of our being.

Each journey comes down to the choices we make as the weeks, months, and years pass. Daily choices such as how to fill the empty hours; mundane choices such as what and when to eat when we don't feel like anything more than a strong cup of coffee or a sleeve of cookies; pivotal choices such as housing, finances, or making our own end-of-life decisions.

Caring for oneself can be exhausting, and yet, possibly the single most important lesson I learned in those first two years was that the ball was firmly in my court. No one was coming to rescue me; no one was waiting in the wings ready for me to pass the torch while I wallowed for awhile in my own misery.

Throughout these pages I have given a great deal of credit to Larry as my spiritual hero, but the truth is the choices I made were mine—as were the missteps. I think sometimes about other relationships I have observed that, while as long-lived as mine was with Larry, are far less intertwined. From time to time, I try placing myself in those circumstances, and I see that whatever the closeness in life, death shatters that bond and one of the two is left to find a way to live on.

Others will move on ... and so will you

Possibly the toughest stumbling block to overcome, even now after nearly a decade, is letting go of the idea that I am the wounded party. There are still days when I want that hero, when I am deeply hurt when others fail to think to include me in some activity, and when I am so very tired of always needing to be the one to step up and make my life happen.

The solution to such bouts of wallowing and inner whining is usually to look for some distraction. I take a walk or focus my attention on small tasks I have postponed or ignored—housework, gardening, bill-paying. Far more effective though are those times when I remind myself that I have not exactly stepped up for others I know are also dealing with tough stuff.

When did I last call or email the friend who is on her second round of chemo? Did I ever follow through on my intention to send that latest Louise Penny novel to my sister? What about the project I started to improve life here in my community that has fallen by the wayside for lack of my involvement?

Robert Kennedy once said, "Some . . . see things as they are and say why. I dream of things that never were and say why not." Having lived by this mantra for some time, these days I find I paraphrase it and say: *Some ask Who will be there for me? while I ask How can I be there for others?*

Feeling sorry for myself comes naturally; reaching out to others takes work. But the rewards are always worth it.

That said, I continue to make mistakes.

You will too.

Big deal. So, you tried something that didn't work. At least you tried. The adage about "if at first you don't succeed," achieved adage-status for a reason. The solution, as I learned, is indeed to try again.

What these years have taught me is that there will probably always be those moments that crop up when I least expect them, when I will feel abandoned and neglected by others. As recently as a few days ago as I write this, I learned that two couples Larry and I used to do lots of things with—people I still see as individuals on a fairly regular basis—had dinner together to celebrate one person's birthday.

I was deeply hurt, especially remembering all the birthdays we had celebrated with dinners together before Larry died. My immediate reaction was to take the fact they had not included me very personally. That they had deliberately excluded me seemed the only possible explanation. After all, over time I had hinted that should they plan to attend events we once attended together, I would love to go along.

But then I reminded myself of how often I had been out of town over the last several years and unavailable for these gatherings. I realized they had continued being together—without me. Bonds had been strengthened. There was no malice in the oversight, and on further introspection, I realized if I had said I'd love to come along when my friend mentioned the dinner, I would have immediately been included. For that matter I was well aware it was this friend's birthday. In the past wouldn't I have been proactive and asked about a possible celebratory get-together?

Of course, the key to the if-at-first-you-don't-succeed adage is to *not* repeat the same mistake. It took me some time to accept that an invitation might not be returned simply because I had reached out. Time and again, it wasn't. And it was months (perhaps even years) before I understood that the return on that investment of my time and effort and hospitality lay not in the idea that such efforts would automatically be duplicated by others at some point in the future. The return came in the form of the pleasure I received in that moment. The reward was in the fact that I had wanted and needed something and instead of waiting for others to deliver, I had made it happen—for both parties.

So, once again I had to face the hard truth that shaping this new life is up to me—not others. I cannot hold my friends responsible for my feelings. They are not mind readers. We cannot change others—only ourselves.

Time wasted

This is a biggie. Certainly, before Larry died—in those months when we knew what was coming—I wasted so many precious hours. Instead of building the memories that might sustain me once he was gone, I languished in feelings of self-pity far too often. Those are moments I can never get back.

Over the decade plus that has passed since, I have spent many moments wandering from room to room of my dwelling of the moment with no purpose, no thought of some purpose—just mindless pacing to try and calm an inner ruckus of feelings of inadequacy, lost opportunities, exhaustion at the constant hard work of moving forward. Literally hours that I could have been working on my next novel or talking to friends or reaching out to someone in need of a virtual hug.

And yet....

As the years have passed and as I have gained confidence in

my ability to make a life without Larry, I have come to see these moments as sometimes necessary. Definitely, not the beating myself up piece of it, but there is value in stepping away from time to time. There is healing in admitting I can't do it all, can't be constantly "on." Sometimes acknowledging pain and loneliness and hurt feelings can actually be therapeutic if my inner poor-me-rant ends at the same place: *So, what are you going to do about it?*

I am by nature a person who fixes things—certainly for others, and now increasingly for myself. In the debate of fight or flight, almost every time I will eventually choose to fight. I certainly don't know enough about psychology to understand if my position as next to youngest in a flock of four siblings has had an effect, but I do know that as far back as I can remember I had a need to make things right—better. Seeing someone I loved suffering physically or emotionally was not something I was willing to observe without trying to change that. Sometimes it worked; sometimes it didn't. So now that I am the one in need, what do I do?

I pace.

I wallow.

I rage.

But in the quieter moments, I recognize the futility of all that, and I turn my focus to fighting back and overcoming. Over time I have realized that fighting for someone else is far easier than fighting for myself. It is then that I turn to others—sometimes a professional therapist; sometimes a really good friend—to walk through this valley of despair with me until I am strong enough to continue on my own. And it occurs to me that this willingness to reach out and allow others to help or to just be still and wait is part of the fight.

To refuse would be textbook flight.

Eating, exercising, and...

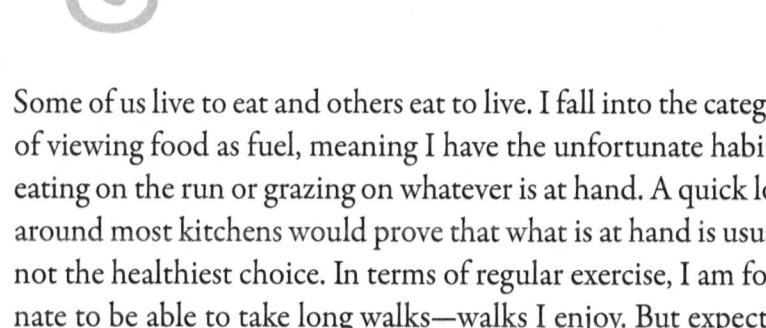

Some of us live to eat and others eat to live. I fall into the category of viewing food as fuel, meaning I have the unfortunate habit of eating on the run or grazing on whatever is at hand. A quick look around most kitchens would prove that what is at hand is usually not the healthiest choice. In terms of regular exercise, I am fortunate to be able to take long walks—walks I enjoy. But expecting me to maintain a regular regimen of cardio or strength-building exercises is like expecting me to go from walking a few miles each day to running a marathon. It will not happen.

That said, it would be foolish of me to even attempt to offer guidance of advice on nutrition and fitness—so I won't. What I will say is for me it has been a constant battle against the appeal of comfort food and surrendering to emotional exhaustion by lying in bed long after I should be up and active. But I am determined to fight that battle. Early on, I fought it because I knew Larry would be so disappointed in me. Now, I fight for me—for the possibility that by doing the right things for my health at least half the time, I will secure myself more time to explore the new and adventurous life I have created.

If I can offer any advice, it's to take the time to attend to the issues in these areas you may have postponed or outright ignored over the last weeks and months. I have finally realized that my best defense against my anxiety and fear that something might happen is to make sure I am doing what I can to prevent that. For example, I have regular check-ups with a primary care doctor I trust—one who listens and is solution-focused. The nutrition thing is, sadly, still a work in progress, but I get kudos from my doctor for being proactive about my health in general.

Mental and emotional health...
not to be ignored

If you've read this far, you already know how sometimes I depended on a therapist to "talk" me down from some crisis or deep dive into depression. My sessions these days are more infrequent, but I continue to value that safety net.

If Larry's mantra was "It is what it is," mine has increasingly become "The only person I can change is myself."

That's been a hard one to learn. Early on I sat back and waited for others to step forward and make things better for me. Often, I was deeply hurt—and sometimes downright angry—when that didn't happen.

There were moments when I sulked and cried, but over time those came less often.

The "W" Word

These days I rely on my mantra and sometimes my therapist to keep me on track. These days I find that I have far happier and rewarding days than I did in those first months and years after Larry died. Reminding myself from time to time of all I have accomplished and done to build a life without him brings its own reward.

Living in the moment

I'm not good at this. I'm working hard to be better, but clearly, I'm a slow learner. I tend to look ahead, always seeking what might lie in the future. I am a procrastinator who gets stuff done. The problem is I tend to skew my priorities toward what I might be able to do quickly or without much planning or thinking. I make lists and somewhere on that list will be a reminder to tend to the writing project at hand or to make a needed medical appointment or to go to the gym—all items that no doubt should come near or at the top of the list. And my intentions are good, but invariably those things get pushed along while I tend to the more mundane items. I'll just make that trip to the market and then get back to writing. Or I'll contact the doctor/dentist as soon as I finish playing this online game. Or I've been on my feet and moving all day. Do I really need to go to the gym?

But while I may not have made much progress when it comes to a list of to-do items, I have made significant strides in terms of my ability to live in the moment when it comes to emotional and mental stress. As I have traveled this avenue of grief and re-creating myself, I find that, without intent, I have changed. These days when I am faced with a conversation or personal interaction that once would have played on my mind for hours and even days after, I am able to look at the situation more rationally. Did I do my best? Is there anything I might do to follow up with the other person? Do I need to apologize or perhaps take the first step toward reconciliation? In the past I would have wallowed in my hurt feelings or anger. But what grief has taught me is that life is way shorter than we expect, and opportunity is there in the moment. It does not hang around. So, perhaps on some level, I have indeed embraced living in the moment.

As for that to-do list? I keep trying.

Guilt

For someone in mourning, guilt comes in many forms. There is, of course, survivor guilt—why him or her and not me? But it also touches every aspect of recovery. I vividly recall at the reception following Larry's memorial, how there were times I caught myself not only smiling but laughing out loud.

How dare I! Others assured me it was shock. Notice they did not reassure me that it was okay—they offered an excuse.

As time passed and I made the decisions that slowly changed my life from one half of a dynamic duo to flying solo, the guilt I felt was another form of survivor guilt. The more content I became with my life, the more shame I felt. What right did I have to this newfound happiness? Friends confirmed my right by repeatedly telling me how excited Larry would have been for me.

One of the hardest things for me during the forty-plus years Larry and I were together was his total disinterest in receiving gifts. For someone like me who grew up in a family where a gift was the expression of love, I had nowhere to go. I had some victories over time—I took us to the Rose Bowl one year and to the NCAA Finals when our team won the championship. But I was never able to stop seeking the perfect gift—the one that would once and for all let him know how very much I loved him.

And then about two years into my journey after he died, I realized the perfect gift—the *only* gift he ever wanted—was for me to live my best life. And so, every day I work hard at doing just that. Most days I am successful. Some days I fail miserably, but as the years have passed, those have become far fewer. More and more, I realize how I honor his memory and the life he led by appreciating the life I have found without him.

Talking about it

As I have mentioned often, talk therapy has gotten me through a lot of rough times. The truth is there was a time when it probably saved our marriage. It was definitely one of my go-to places for solace and counsel during the last months of Larry's life, and even after all this time, it is something I find comfort in knowing is there for me. It has become a key tool in my ability to deal with longstanding issues like loneliness and self-doubt, as well as newer trials such as facing old age and the myriad of fears and challenges that come with that.

Full disclosure: it took a lot of trial and error before I connected with the therapist who became my guide. There were a couple of nightmarish encounters with therapists who seemed more interested in telling me their problems than letting me talk about mine. There was one who felt she had all the answers and if I would just listen to her, life would be perfect. She did most of the talking during our sessions. I also tried support groups, and quickly learned I was not a "group" person. I came from a family who viewed the need for any sort of emotional or mental healing as a weakness and something to be avoided at all costs. With that upbringing, I had prolonged periods where I was determined to "fix" myself, but finally had to admit I could not do this alone.

The point is I did not admit defeat. I kept trying and finally found the right connection. How do you go about finding that connection?

There are several places you can start: ask your primary care doctor for a referral; try a support group for widows and widowers; talk to your pastor, rabbi or preferred religious contact. There is a good possibility you may have insurance coverage for treatment. And remember, the professional you choose is bound by the same HIPPA rules your primary care physician and other doctors follow.

Most of all, understand that *you* are in charge. If one encounter does not work out, you do not need to stay with that, but keep looking. Just remember, unless your friend or family member is a trained counselor and you are prepared to put that relationship on a different footing, choosing someone new to you (and you to them) gives you a win-win. You have a trusted therapist and your relationship with that friend or family member benefits from the insights you gain as you find your way.

That said, there are alternative possibilities for dealing with mental and emotional stress. Some—such as self-medication and alcohol—can do more harm than good. But there are others. Meditation works for some. Physical activity and practices such as yoga and tai chi may also prove helpful. Maybe try a combination of professional and alternative therapies. The important thing to keep in mind is that this is your life—you are in control.

Control

And speaking of control, remember the maxim I mentioned earlier? The one about how the only person you can change is *you*? That also holds true for control.

Just as you can't change another person's behavior, you cannot control their responses or actions. Control is about choice—the choices we make throughout our lives. If another person misinterprets something you say, that's not something you can control—you can try and explain the mistaken impression, but only the other person can control how that explanation is accepted. Similarly, only you have control over feelings generated by others.

What I've learned—sometimes the hard way—is that I may need to take time to examine those feelings before reacting. For someone widowed recently (or even years ago), trusting that others might not have meant a comment or action to cause hurt feelings may not come easily.

Preparing for what comes next

Real control comes with preparation. Taking charge of those aspects of life it is possible to direct. Getting your house in order, so to speak. Do you have a power of attorney in place? For both healthcare and for financial decisions? When's the last time you took a look at your will? Do you even have a will? If so, some decisions and choices you made when your partner was living may no longer be valid.

And then there is your financial future—what does that look like? It's vital that you take a long view of this. Consider what your income and expenses are likely to be for the coming years. Then think about how things might change if you became ill or lost your job or the market tanked.

I was fortunate to already have in place professionals who could walk me through all this—a financial planner, the attorney who would handle my estate once I died, and trusted friends I could rely on for sound advice and guidance. We had invested in long-term care insurance years earlier, and now I had that cushion to soften the blow of any unforeseen ongoing health issues.

And once again, I understand that my circumstances are not yours. But even those in reduced circumstances have experts they can rely on. If you have a bank account, then you have a bank with people trained in helping you manage even limited assets. If your community has a public or university library, you have access to librarians who can guide you to resources available there. If your community offers adult learning, look for classes on planning your retirement or managing your finances—and sign up. If you can afford the services of an elder law attorney trained specifically in the areas of estate and retirement planning, do so.

Finally, a word about doing your research online: *be careful!* As with any topic today, there is a lot of bad and misinformation out there offered by people out to scam you or who have a higher than they should opinion of their qualifications to offer advice. Choose sites that end in .edu or .gov rather than ones that are basic .com.

And question everything.

Unexpected tears

After nearly a decade, these still creep up on me when I am least prepared for them. Last Christmas I was co-chairing a holiday celebration at the senior community where I live. The event had multiple moving pieces—a bazaar, a raffle, a choir concert, and more. I was standing outside the hall where the choir was performing, listening as they ran through the usual litany of carols. I hummed along, warm in the memories triggered of childhood Christmas pageants and adult candlelight services. And then the director announced they would close with *Silent Night*.

The pianist played the introduction and the choir and audience had not even made it to ... *holy night*, when I realized I was crying—actually closer to sobbing. I made a quick getaway down the hall to a deserted part of the building to compose myself. I had no explanation—no specific memory I could connect to having that reaction to that carol. It's not even my favorite.

And yet several minutes passed before I was able to rejoin the festivities.

There have been other instances, equally surprising and bewildering—a television commercial; a sappy movie; the sight of an older couple walking hand in hand in the park.

Darn it, I'm choking up now!

But these days, while I may not relish especially a public breakdown, I do understand the healing power of these moments—the emotional release that tells me perhaps I have not been paying close attention to the need to sometimes take a step away and reflect on the choices I have made along the way and consider what I might need to change as I continue to move forward.

Old traditions updated

If you and your partner were together for years—decades even, there were certain traditions you slid into over that time. A certain way even mundane things were done like the way one of you loaded the dishwasher or folded the socks. There were also special occasion traditions such as routines that were part of holidays. Earlier I talked about a tradition Larry and I had of taking a drive to look at holiday lights in December while singing along to music blasting from the car's CD player.

You may recall that when I decided to continue that tradition after Larry died, it did not work for several reasons—I was in Florida, few houses were decorated, and most of all, I was alone. I quickly realized I could not recreate something just the two of us had originated.

With a little updating, other traditions worked. For example, even when I traveled alone, but as part of a tour group, I still went off on my own at times and came back to the group later to relate the adventure I'd had... just as I used to do when Larry and I traveled. Of course, I missed the way he would laugh or commiserate with an adventure gone wrong, but in most cases I got those reactions in different forms from my fellow travelers. I began to delight in a newfound appreciation that I could make others laugh or at least find pleasure in the moment.

I have heard of some who abandon all the traditions they built through the years with their partner. "It's just too painful," they might say. And I can understand that. But to cast everything aside without at least experimenting with ways it might be possible to sustain the tradition and gain the comfort and solace it once brought seems to me to be an exercise in atonement for something that was never that person's fault.

I no longer take that Christmas Eve car ride, but I continue to love the inventive ways people find to light up the season, so if I am going somewhere in December after dark, I will choose the route that is most likely to take me through neighborhoods festooned for the season. In short, I avoid the highway—the quicker way—and take the side road more likely to reveal something unexpected.

Don't try going it alone...
Say "Yes" more often than "No"

As established, I am by nature fiercely independent and a loner with a tendency to believe I can manage on my own. But here is perhaps one of the most important lessons I have learned over the last decade without Larry: a person needs fuel—physical, mental, and emotional.

Diet and exercise are key, of course. But the power of new information, new ideas, new PEOPLE cannot be underestimated as a healing force. How you choose to bring those elements of mental and emotional nutrition and stimulation into your life will vary greatly from the ways I have done that. But the results can be amazing.

An evening spent with friends is far more likely to feed you with laughter and sharing and perhaps new insights about how you might move forward than curling up on the sofa alone with the TV on. Joining a book club through your local library or bookstore can bring the double bonus of meeting some new people and having the mental stimulation of learning something through discussion.

And most of all, accepting help when it is offered by understanding it is not being offered out of pity, but genuine concern carries a special gift. By allowing others to show their love and friendship, you are the giver as well as the recipient.

Giving up is NOT an option

We can't know what tomorrow or next week or next year might bring. We can probably safely predict that not every day will bring seashells and balloons. But now and again—in my case when trying to stay constantly positive and upbeat became beyond exhausting—a miracle might just happen.

A couple of years ago, when I was frankly depressed and overcome with self-pity that bordered on depression, I opened my mail one day to find a photograph of a young man looking out at the world with my father's twinkling eyes and half smile. Half a century earlier I had gotten pregnant with no job and no prospects and had given my child up for adoption.

Through the decades that followed I thought of him constantly as Larry (who was not the father) and I found our way through miscarriages and the ultimate decision to not have children. Those years filled with attending the passages of the children of our friends—and then on to their grandchildren. Over time I had brief communication with the doctor who had delivered my son and arranged the adoption and so was fairly certain all was well. Often, I wrestled with wanting to meet him but saw that as selfish on my part when I knew he had found a good life with caring parents. I settled for letting the doctor know how to contact me should my son need me.

Fast forward to that photo and note that arrived at a time when I was struggling to stay afloat . . . my son wanted to know if I might be open to starting a conversation.

Would I ever!

We began with emails and handwritten letters and then came phone calls. Then COVID hit so we finally met in person via Zoom. I have a daughter-in-law—a beautiful soul who clearly loves my son. No grandchildren, but in some ways that was a relief because I wanted to focus on him.

A couple of months ago as I write this, we finally met in person in Chicago where he'd grown up a mere ninety miles from my home in Milwaukee. It's weird to say this, but thanks to COVID we'd had time to get to know each other a bit so that this in-person meeting was nowhere near as awkward as it might have been. We walked and talked and laughed and revealed stories of our pasts. He showed me landmarks of his youth. We found trivial things we share in common—both find umbrellas annoying; both like to get to airports early and wait there instead of waiting at home. We made plans for me to visit for the holidays.

And through it all I have felt Larry's spirit sharing his delight for my joy in finding this family I never thought I would know. And every time my son calls me "Mom" and ends a call or letter with his love, I understand that while my journey *through* is not yet over and I have relied heavily on Larry's spirit to travel with me, these days I have my son as well.

My charge to you is to look for the signs—look for the miracles—large and small. You can make this journey your journey, unique in all the ways you are. And you can do that with grace and laughter and tears.

One day you will realize that you have done your best to honor the person you shared life with before while building for yourself a new normal filled with purpose—and even a new definition of happiness.

About the Author

Jo Horne is the award-winning author of over forty works of fiction and non-fiction. A former marketing and communications professional for two international corporations who has also taught at the college level and run a mom-and-pop adult daycare business with her husband, Jo is now retired and focused only on writing. She splits her time between Wisconsin and Florida.

www.ingramcontent.com/pod-product-compliance
Lightning Source LLC
Chambersburg PA
CBHW020525080526
44583CB00013B/740